INT
CONSCIOUSNESS
AND SPORT

UNIFYING BODY, MIND AND SPIRIT THROUGH FLOW

A Model. A Process. A Practice.

SCOTT FORD

outskirtspress

DENVER, COLORADO

Outskirts Press, Inc.
http://www.outskirtspress.com

ISBN: 978-1-4787-6926-2

Outskirts Press and the "OP" logo are trademarks belonging to Outskirts Press, Inc.

PRINTED IN THE UNITED STATES OF AMERICA

About Integral Consciousness and Sport

Unity of Being, the coming together in action of all dimensions of Self – called Flow or the Zone is the allure and Holy Grail of the Athletic Experience. From this Unity state comes peak experience and ecstatic enjoyment of our sport. We have touched the Divine. All who have participated in sport have felt it.

This typically vividly remembered, elusive, yet profound state of Experience has been thought to be accidental, certainly unpredictable, eliciting the comment, "if I could bottle it I'd be a billionaire."

Guess what. Master tennis coach Scott Ford in this extraordinary book shows us how to get there, a predictable way to drop into this Unity state of consciousness and awareness - the Zone. As Scott points out, we have a choice in the matter.

Scott's journey of discovery, his Eureka moment and the courage to pursue and develop this discovery, often times against the grain of more traditional ways of coaching, over the past 40 years is a wonderful story in itself.

As a former professional athlete, where the Flow/Zone state is often experienced, but typically not talked about, I highly recommend this marvelous book to all athletes. The Flow/Zone state is always right in front of us, it is a question how to gain access. Scott Ford shows us how.

David Meggyesy
St. Louis football Cardinals -- 1963-69
Founding Member: Sports, Energy, and Consciousness Group
Author: *Out of Their League*

* * *

This book is a very persuasive demonstration of Ford's central thesis: that a shift in exterior mode of operation leads to a shift in interior state of consciousness. That may sound like the tail is wagging the dog, because biomechanics won't get you into the Zone, but the reader will be rewarded with a fascinating tour of the metaphysics of sport.

Scott Ford is a mystic disguised as a tennis coach, with a little bit of neuroscientist and sports psychologist thrown in for good measure. I'm not sure why he isn't famous, because he can reliably improve anyone's game while simultaneously opening them to the wonder of the Infinite Present. That is no small thing, and this book is a wonderful map to getting there.

Eric Leskowitz, M.D.
Dept. of Psychiatry, Harvard Medical School
Founding Member: Sports, Energy, and Consciousness Group

* * *

I've been fortunate enough to have read and learnt from Scott Ford's earlier works, "Design B" and "Welcome to the Zone". I was mistakenly under the impression that I know enough about The Zone... and had actually no inclination to read anything further that is related to this topic.

Then, a PDF on Scott's new book: "Integral Consciousness & Sport" fell on my lap. It is my good fortune that I intuitively read it with new-found enthusiasm and verve. And what a treat!

Scott is a Master Teacher. He has demonstrated in engaging detail what we can do not only to prepare for flow but also what we can do to intentionally create a flow state. To me, this is the way to ease into "effortless effort" and to know with a high degree of confidence that we will succeed.

Integral Consciousness and Sport shows us how to delve into our Higher Self and become Limitless. I firmly believe that every sport coach worth their salt, should make it a point to read this book now, or at least, sometime in the course of their coaching career."

Desmond Oon, Ph.D.
Master Professional, USPTA
Author: *Can Eastern Wisdom Improve Your Tennis? Soft Tennis & Conversation with a Zen Tennis Master*
Creator: "Spiritual Tennis" workshops & seminars

* * *

As a former professional lacrosse goalie in Major League Lacrosse, I was having trouble "seeing" a little rubber orange ball that could be launched at me upwards of 115 miles per hour from three to 15 yards in front of me. So, I went to Scott Ford for what I thought would simply be a physical exercise in learning to use my eyes in a more efficient way. While he taught me that, I learned way more about myself than I could have ever bargained for.

Ford's method to assist people to enter "the flow state" or "the zone" in athletics is extremely powerful and effective. It helps athletes to become more present, let go of egotistical hang-ups, and become completely one with their experience. This not only allows athletes to perform at higher levels than they have ever imagined, but it also provides them with an opportunity to enjoy their sport more fully than ever before.

On top of all this, athletes will take the lessons that they learn from the transformational experience of being in flow with them into their everyday lives to become better partners, parents, friends, and contributing members of society. Ford has dedicated his entire life to high-performance athletics, self-development, and spirituality and this book ties all of that together in a powerful manner that will leave a lasting mark on athletes for generations to come.

Trevor Tierney
Co-founder and Vice-President of Icon Lacrosse
Former winner of NCAA Championship,
International Lacrosse Federation World Championship,
and Major League Lacrosse Championship.

* * *

Do you dream of the 'perfect' match or game, where you compete to your highest potential and enter the Zone? Now imagine there is a coach who can teach you how to step into that dream on your own on a regular basis. Reading *Integral Consciousness in Sport* is like sitting down with that coach for the biggest "AHA!" of your life.

Scott causally distills his powerful insights into relevant and easy to apply real-world concepts that will change far more than your game. Are you ready for a whole new level of performance? Your own peak performance in sport and in life? Read this book, apply the concepts, practice them and prepare to see more than your game start to shift!"

Heidi McCoy and Josh Crist, Martial Arts Instructors

* * *

Scott Ford is a transformative tennis professional. Taking a lesson from him (or reading this book) will improve your game and influence your life as well. When your mind and spirit are revitalized by his Parallel Mode Process, the simple act of 'seeing 'the tennis ball come towards you can change your perspective on the game, and on life itself.

Michael Spino, Ph.D.
Founding Member, Sports, Energy, and Consciousness Group
Author: *Beyond Jogging: The Inner Spaces of Running*

* * *

Scott Ford practices and writes, "everyone is capable of playing their chosen sport in a state of flow: everyone is capable of creating a unified reality with their athletic environment, but because we are so conditioned to dualistic thinking, subject-object thinking, we find it difficult to shift out of this dualistic mindset."

For years I have been trying to find out how you can create flow, and now, for the first time, Scott has clearly outlined the process. This is a significant breakthrough for all athletes in all sports; the Parallel Mode Process is a step forward in the evolution of sport. I have had athletes on a number of occasions tell me that they had experienced the effortless flow state, but until Scott's excellent book it was all a mystery as to how it was achieved.

Now I am trying to do the same for rowing as Scott has done for tennis. I like the idea that he has probed deeply, deep psychology at work here. It is truly an inspirational piece of writing and, most importantly, a worthy practice.

Jimmy Joy
Author: *The Joy of Sculling* and *The Quantum Sculler*

* * *

And this from Dr. Damien Lafont:

Since the very beginning, and later when I met him Denver in 2008, I always felt there was something different, something profound in Scott's work. Now, after spending the last twenty years studying the flow and how to access it, I can say with no doubt that Scott's lifetime work is brilliant and revolutionary in the fields of sport, human potential and consciousness. It will become a reference work in the emerging field of sport and spirituality.

First, if you're performance-oriented, you will discover in Scott's earlier book, "Welcome to the Zone," that when focusing on your contact zone your response time is three to five times faster than your normal response times! This is awesome, but it's only one dimension of Scott's work. If, like many people, you are looking for something more in your sport, in your life, with this book, you will see there is much more in tennis than just hitting a tennis ball. Scott opens an entire new world where you have to drop your old ideas about what's possible and what's not, about what you can do and what you can't. Scott offers the first deep reflexion about the spatiotemporal dimension of flow, and beyond tennis itself, you will find here a totally new approach to the athlete and his environment.

You'll also find everything you need to access a higher state of consciousness and maybe experience for a moment or more your true nature as human being – all of this through sport! How is that possible? The answer is: Scott takes us back to the present. And more than anything else, presence is what we need. Not only to perform at our best, but firstly to live better, to live our true nature and full potential.

To be honest, I don't think Scott's work is really about sport or peak performance. It's actually about "flowing presence." Everything happens in the present. It seems basic, but we often get into big trouble because we forget this simple truth. Being in the zone is therefore being present in the unfolding flow. As Scott says, "Presence IS the Zone". So, finding the zone is naturally finding your way back to the flowing presence.

There are, of course, different ways to access the present moment, and Scott points out one of them - a new, dynamic and effective way to access presence. Scott is not the only one who tried to find the secret to flowing presence, and the researchers have faced a big wall trying to solve the mystery of flow, finally concluding the best you can hope for is to create the conditions of flow. With such a consensus of opinion, everybody stopped at flow.

Not Scott! And that's what I really like in his approach – no matter the conclusion of the experts – he asked the right question: What can we do to intentionally create a flow state? Yes, you've read well – *intentionally* create a flow state. Powerful. So powerful that you won't be surprised to learn that several research groups, mainly in the US, are currently working on these questions. They understand the immense applications in human performance for sport, business or military purpose. With the help of the recent developments of neuroscience, they put all their effort to find the code to create the flow at will. But they are still searching …

That's where Scott took a decisive turn before everybody. From his personal experience, he knew that our attention has something to do with the zone. So he naturally asked a more precise question: What attentional pattern is necessary for peak performance? The answer: We need a shift of attention – a shift made consciously, intentionally. This approach requires a completely different visual strategy centred on the contact zone: Focusing your eyes, your attention, your thought and your mind on what you really want: your contact.

Indeed, the most important and decisive event in fast-ball sports like tennis or baseball is contact. So everything you learn about your sport should be to toward the best contact possible. That's precisely Scott's approach. To focus your eyes *and* your mind. That's, in fact, a huge statement. And that's where Scott is a pioneer. Until now, not only have we been taught to focus our eyes on the ball, we have also been taught to focus our minds on the ball – and that's the origin of all troubles.

Focusing on the ball will never tell you what to do, how to position your body, where to put your racquet. When you focus your mind on contact, you create a clear image, then your body naturally follows. That's total trust in your body's capacity to do a complex task without you thinking of every single detail. Of course, focusing on the contact zone, this empty space, may be confronting because it goes against what you know about your sport. Is fixing your focus on the empty space of your contact zone focusing on nothing? Not really, you focus on the contact. You focus on what you want to achieve. And concentration on what you really want, what you truly desire is always how you progress and get results.

Everything in our reality starts from a thought, an idea, and an image in our mind. Focusing our mind on the right thing is always how we create and change our reality. Here, this power thought is your contact zone, your contact point, the optimum one. Focusing on what you want is the Parallel Mode Process – the flow is the effect. Cause and Effect. Simple. Yes your will can take you to the flow.

Of course, what is simple is often dismissed because people's conditioning asks for heavy, man-made, scientific techniques. You have to work hard to maybe, by chance, one day access flow. You have to deserve the zone. But is it true? The answer is no. Scott shows that you can forget chance, coincidence, and the 10,000 hours of practice. In short, forget everything you've learned about the flow.

While the leading edge researchers are working hard to hack the flow, we are stuck in the old thinking of necessary hard labour and suffering to access the zone. We struggle, we doubt and often accept the idea that it's not for us. We know it's there, somewhere, but it seems we can't access it. This moment when everything comes together. This moment we are waiting for but that never comes. We know it's there, right there. It's so close, sometimes we can feel it. And that's why we get so frustrated, feeling unfulfilled, uncompleted – we know it's here but we can't find the key! It's too hard, requires too much effort, therefore only the lucky ones, talented athletes or brilliant minds can experience it. Here, the good news is that Scott gives you one key to access this part of you, you're relentlessly seeking.

Beyond presence, Scott's work is also about the power of thoughts, the power of will and concentration. The ability to concentrate and hold the attention upon any given point at will, and resist all distractions is an absolute necessity to high performance and rapid progress. Happily you can acquire this art, and the very practice itself is a wholesome and efficient mental discipline. Have something to do, and do it! That's mental concentration. Concentration is only paying attention to right thoughts – and the right thought in tennis is 'positive contact'. Thus, applying Scott's method, you can rise from habit formed through neglect or necessity, to a habit formed because you desire and choose it. Shifting your attention and concentrate on what really matters. That's one of the main teachings in this book.

However, we have not been trained to choose our thoughts, and are too much of the time subject to wandering. The Parallel Mode Process is voluntary concentration. It is wilful concentration. It is concentration upon a chosen thought. It is doing voluntarily and with a determined purpose that which you have been letting yourself do involuntarily all your life. Here we talk about the *intentional* creation of your peak performance state. Yes this idea goes against all the sport psychology theories insisting that you cannot *intentionally* create flow.

The truth is you can. Flow is always available to you – because the present is always available! Every moment in your life, you can be fully present in the flow state and experience the zone. Everybody can access these moments. Everybody has the potential to be more present. And to develop this practice of presence, tennis has something special: the repetitive nature of actions – hitting the ball again, again and again. That's the genius of Scott – using the repetitive nature of tennis as a means to create the flow, and enter *your* zone.

Truth is identical whether uttered by ancient or modern teacher, no matter what form their teaching takes. For Scott it happened to be tennis – for others it is dance, music or science. The door is not really important. What matters the most is what is beyond the door; what is always here, always accessible, always present.

Here you think you play tennis but you are back home – back to the present! Suddenly, sport becomes a vehicle for awakening to your own true nature. Yes, Scott's teaching is a spiritual practice disguised as a sport. The student does the work, walks a new path without realizing it. That's the ultimate teaching. That's also the mark of great teachers.

We are living an exciting time in human development, and it's an exciting time for you because this book – if you are ready - will guide you to the path of oneness with the present moment as it unfolds, and this will change your life. You just have to be willing to change. Scott simply shows us how an activity like tennis, how sport in general, can be the door to deeper meaning and higher levels of consciousness. But to open the door, you need to have the will to enter. It's a choice. Your choice. That's the revolutionary idea here, we have the choice to enter, and we have the power to be present, to be *Presence* – consciously.

Damien Lafont, PhD

Melbourne, Australia, December, 5th 2015.

Author of *"Back to the Zone - Sport and Inner Experiences"* (2012)

and co-author of *"Your True Nature - wisdom of living masters"* (2014)

Acknowledgements

I would like to thank several people who have helped me to continue my journey into higher consciousness and flow in sports. Lee Elliott, USPTA, for her encouragement and support in providing an open-minded atmosphere in which to teach the Parallel Mode Process. Drs. Michael and Karin Mesches of SciTechEdit International for their editorial assistance throughout the book. The graphics team of Cindy Sewick, Sara Ford, and Tyler Ford for the cover design and interior graphics. And finally, to my wife Jane for walking the path with me.

Table of Contents

Foreword

By Ken Wilber

States of consciousness are a key component of the Integral Model and an Integral Life Practice, and I believe Scott Ford has discovered a truly new, novel, and effective way to access a profound state of unity consciousness, also called "integral consciousness" —the kind of state you'd expect from meditative and contemplative spiritual training. But Scott isn't a spiritual teacher; he's a Tennis Teaching Professional. In his "day job" Scott is a Peak Performance Specialist at a tennis club in Colorado, and he markets his teaching as "Tennis in the Zone."

For the modern-rational segment of the population that believes only in scientific materialism, "spiritual states of consciousness" are, at best, the epiphenomenon of neurons in the brain misfiring in a particularly unfortunate way. For this strictly empirical worldview, having a direct experience of Infinity and having a psychotic break are generally seen as equally aberrant experiences deserving of medical intervention. Hence, for most of his professional career Scott has described his work as getting people in touch with "the zone," rather than getting people in touch with Spirit.

The remarkable fact is, based on a practice he stumbled upon and then refined for over three decades, Scott has come to know Spirit quite well. As much as Scott loves introducing people to their athletic peak performance state, introducing people to their own deepest dimensions of being and reality is much more rewarding. This is the purpose of the book you now hold in your hands. So what's the practice, and how does it work? It's called the Parallel Mode Process (PMP), and it all takes place in the present, so that is where we will start.

The great contemplative spiritual traditions of the world are unanimous in asserting that the present holds the key to realizing the nature of ultimate reality or Spirit. They maintain that this ultimate or absolute reality must be entirely and fully present in all moments, and that there are no moments in time that are "more real" or "closer to" Spirit than other moments. Spirit, to be truly absolute and infinite, must be 100% present at all times without exception. In fact, these traditions maintain that Spirit *transcends* time entirely, and is itself timeless and eternal. Spirit was there *before* time began—before the Big Bang—and so it must be equally and entirely present at all points in time. Therefore, if you desire to know Spirit, you need only examine this present moment. To look anywhere else is to assure you will *always* miss that which is *always* present.

The Christian mystics maintain that there are at least two major ways to define what we mean by "the present." They refer to these distinctions as the *nunc fluens* and the *nunc stans*. The *nunc fluens* is the "passing present" in which most people feel they live their lives. The 2-3 second gap between past and future in which all experience unfolds. This passing present can also be seen as the "flowing present," as time can always be felt as flowing from past to present to future. Here, there is always a sense of movement, as if you are standing on a raft, floating naturally and easily with the currents of a vast river.

The *nunc stans* is the "eternal present," and this eternal present is the home of infinite Spirit. The *nunc stans*, as the absolute present, embraces—or transcends and includes—all time as it arises in the *nunc fluens*, or relative present. Here, in the *nunc stans*, you stand free of the movement of time and becoming, the movement of all rivers and rafts, and there is the feeling of utter stillness, immovability, and timelessness.

In the course of meditative or contemplative training, the great mystical traditions will invariably teach their students how to rest within the passing present before they attempt to point out the eternal present. Students will be taught concentrative exercises designed to rein in their wandering attention from flights of thought into the past or future. Maintaining steady moment-to-moment awareness is the task at hand, and often students are taught to simply follow their breath. With practice, students begin to notice that the mind quiets down of its own, the body relaxes, and the breath becomes slow and deep. Most people find they are introduced to a powerful sense of equanimity, peace, and deep contentment. Through effort, concentration, and diligent practice, the body and mind are brought to a state of stillness and deep acceptance of the present moment, *exactly as it is*. This is not itself an awakened or enlightened state, but simply the student ceasing to divert attention into past and future, and finally becoming profoundly **one** with the *nunc fluens*, the flowing present.

As remarkable as unity with the *nunc fluens* is, the enlightenment traditions see this state as a prerequisite for beginning to locate the *nunc stans*. If one cannot peaceably rest in the present moment as it arises and falls, letting all thoughts and sensations be as they are without objection, one's awareness will never be free enough to effectively enquire into the nature of the eternal present. This enquiry has nothing whatsoever to do with effort or concentration, but rather with the *recognition* of Spirit in its timeless dimension. A common practice here is a variation on *neti neti*, which simply means "not this, not that." Students here adopt a position of simply Witnessing all thoughts, emotions, and sensations, and noticing that that which is *aware* of all thoughts, emotions, and sensations is intrinsically *free* of all that. I *have* thoughts, but I am *not* my thoughts. I *have* emotions, but I am *not* my emotions. I *have* sensations, but I am *not* my sensations. If I am "not this, not that," then who am I? Who is this Witness that impartially notices all qualities of experience and yet has none of its own? What is this awareness in me that perfectly mirrors all phenomena without grasping or avoidance?

Gradually, it dawns on practitioners that their own subjectivity, their own IAMness, is without any boundaries whatsoever. All objects that arise in awareness are exactly that: **objects**, and *not* the true **subject**. "I" cannot possibly be any object whatsoever, because objects possess no consciousness, awareness, sentience. With time, it becomes clear that a thought or an emotion is an object in *exactly* the same manner as a rock, a chair, a nose, or a kidney. I may *have* a thought, emotion, rock, chair, nose, or kidney, but I am *not* any of those. Who am I? When one has dis-identified with all objects whatsoever, one experiences what Zen calls "body-mind dropped." You are the Pure Witness, the Absolute Subject, the Infinite I AM. This is your own Buddha Nature, this is your own Christ Consciousness. This is who you were prior to the Big Bang. In fact, this is who you *are* prior to the Big Bang. The Big Bang never happened, not in Truth. In Truth, only vast Emptiness is real, only radically unqualifiable Being is real, only infinite Godhead is real—and I AM That.

The illustrious Hindu sage Ramana Maharshi, echoing Shankara, stated the Truth thusly:

> The world is illusory
> Brahman alone is real

Brahman is the Absolute, the Unqualifiable, the Eternal. But the story does not end here in the Big Empty, because Ramana Maharshi was a profound *nondual* Realizer, and the Truth—the *Whole* Truth—is contained in the capping line of his three-line summary of spiritual understanding:

> Brahman is the world

The nondual traditions, East and West, proclaim in unison that Form and Emptiness are not-two! Form is *exactly* Emptiness and Emptiness is *exactly* Form. There is no duality to be found in Reality. Nirvana and samsara are One, the One without a second. Eternity is in Love with the productions of time, and the Awakened Masters tell us of the Joy and Bliss of this most Holy and Blessed union. There is no struggle, strife, pain, suffering, or injustice *anywhere* in Reality. There is *only* Spirit, and this vast and wondrous Kosmos is but a gesture of infinite Freedom, an ornament of the Eternal. Resting as the eternal present, I cannot help but Love everyone and everything that arises in the passing present, and I feel nothing but perfect Harmony between time and the timeless. There is only Spirit, there is only God, there is only the Absolute. There is only Perfect Unity and Radical Freedom and Divine Delight.

We have travelled from the *nunc fluens* to the *nunc stans* to their ever-present unity as the Nondual, and now we can turn to the topic of this book: Tennis "in the zone" and the Parallel Mode Process. .

As we stated earlier, students of the great Wisdom Traditions must generally demonstrate an ability to be one with the *nunc fluens*—the flowing present—before they are taught how to be one with the *nunc stans*—the absolute present. Typically students are taught forms of silent meditation or contemplation whereby they learn to be attentive to the present moment without grasping or avoiding. These practices are designed to focus and still the mind, the emotions, the body. These practices show you the experience of what it is to be a human being when you are not compulsively ricocheting between past regret and future fear.

One begins to learn that a life lived in the present is a life of flow, and that, remarkably, it is difficult to locate any truly insurmountable problems in the present. Challenges and difficulties can and do arise, and they may alter the course of your life forever, but they no longer have the ability to brutalize you as they did before. By abiding in the present moment, even pain, sickness, and death can be met with equanimity, compassion, and dignity. I discover that as painful, irritating, or boring as the present may be, it is the *avoidance* of the present that causes me to suffer. It is the *resistance* to the present moment which actually generates suffering.

It is monumental when students realize that when they stop avoiding, resisting, and fleeing the present moment, they *stop suffering*. Suffering is created by "moving away" from the present, and the only person who can cause me to "move away" is *me*. I am *entirely* responsible for the causation or cessation of this movement, and it is only with this insight that I can take responsibility for my entire human life and how it affects those around me. The insight that suffering is self-generated is often considered the bedrock of a meditative or contemplative life. This insight is found through the power of *not* "moving away," and by not moving away I find unity with the flowing present, the *nunc fluens*. The monumental realization is that when I stop avoiding and resisting and fleeing the present moment, I *stop suffering*.

As simple as it sounds to "abide always in the present moment," these spiritual disciplines are really and truly *disciplines*, requiring focused practice at least once a day. It can be many months before practitioners experience the clarity, equanimity, and freedom of spiritual practice, and it can be many more years before practitioners have access to this experience with regularity. For this reason, many people simply give up on their practice, or only practice half-heartedly and infrequently. Many people feel that the amount of time and effort they put into their practice relative to the benefits they perceive is just not worth it. It can often feel like an exercise in futility, because the mental and emotional "chatter" familiar to us all simply does not die down by sitting quietly for half an hour every day. It just becomes an acutely aggravating experience of just how distracted and unsatisfied we actually are. And why should I do that to myself every day? I am more aware of my suffering than ever, so screw it!

Observant readers will have noted that I have not mentioned the practices that one does to get in touch with the *absolute* present, and there's a good reason for this—the Great Wisdom Traditions are clear that there is nothing you can **do** to get in touch with the absolute present, which is to say, absolute reality itself. For absolute reality to be truly absolute, it must *always* be 100% present. Trying to locate the absolute present is like trying to locate your foot—it is *always there*, you just have to recognize it. If you start running around looking for your foot, you are significantly less likely to notice it is fully present **right now**.

The ultimate paths of spiritual understanding are in fact paths of recognition. They are not practices because there is nothing to do; there is nothing to "practice." These "paths of recognition" generally consist of various pointing-out instructions, which aim to "point out" the absolute nature of the present moment. But the truth is, most people can't actually rest in the present moment long enough to be able to engage these pointing-out instructions with rigor or clarity. *This is why for every major contemplative tradition students **must** demonstrate the capacity to be stably one with the temporal present **before** pointing out instructions are given.* Unity with the temporal present is not a poor-man's substitute for unity with the absolute present; it is the necessary and unavoidable foundation of every being who has ever Awakened to the Absolute. Therefore, if you want to Wake Up, then (1) create an Integral Life Practice that works for you, (2) find a reputable teacher who specializes in "pointing out" ever-present Spirit, and (3) do whatever you can to learn how to be one with the present moment as it unfolds, enfolds, and flows towards your own ever-present Divinity.

From pre-modernity to the present day, the wisdom traditions have been the creators and custodians of these methods of liberating the human heart and mind – and rightly so. But part of what the modern and postmodern worlds have shown us is that the Kosmos evolves and the modes of Spirit's expression evolve. Just because some extraordinary spiritual souls discovered how to become one with the present—both temporal and absolute—several millennia ago, does not mean theirs will be the only way for the rest of time.

I believe Scott Ford has discovered a truly novel and effective way to access the nunc fluens – unity states with the temporal present. Perhaps, most extraordinary of all, he has made spiritual practice *fun*! Silent, seated meditation may be time-honored and effective, but very few people would call it fun, at least from the perspective of a beginner. No matter how profound a spiritual practice may be, if the student doesn't return to the practice repeatedly over time, they are not going to make much headway. Scott's practice occurs within the context of the game of tennis, so fun is baked into the equation from the beginning—people *want* to come back and play tennis again and again, especially if they can play tennis in the zone!

The other astonishing achievement of the PMP is that it appears to work in *minutes*—not weeks, not months, not years—and there are no special prerequisites whatsoever. Anyone who can hold a racquet can "get in the zone" and learn what it means to be one with the present. Scott has successfully taught the PMP to individuals in wheelchairs and children with learning disabilities as well as elite, professional athletes. You can make this practice as athletic as you want, but you don't have to be an athlete to fully experience its value.

Scott Ford is a Master of unity with the flowing now, and with over three decades of experience worshipping in the temple of the present, the Absolute Now also shines through clearly in his own case. It can be the same for you.

Not all who love Spirit are still and silent. There are those who Dance. There are those who Sing. And there are also those who Play.

How do *you* want to worship today?

Ken Wilber
Denver, CO

An Accidental Awakening

In 1978, at the age of 30, I was ready to give up teaching tennis and look for a "real job." Teaching people how to play tennis had become increasingly boring; the same thing day after day: move your feet this way, grip your racquet that way, turn your shoulders like this, swing your racquet like that…over and over again until I felt like I could teach the game of tennis with my eyes closed – which, I would come to find out, was exactly what I was doing.

On a hot day that summer, I discovered that my eyes had indeed been closed, but not to teaching tennis. Rather, my eyes had been closed to myself, to my real self, to my own true nature as a tennis player, and as a human being. In what I can only describe as an accidental awakening, my eyes were suddenly opened to the authentic reality of my own being.

Here's what happened:

While I was practicing with a friend of mine, I started doing something on the court that was very unlike me, something counterintuitive and quite childlike and imaginative. To my amazement, every time I did this imaginary thing, I found myself shifting from my normal performance state to my peak performance state; what athletes refer to as playing "in the zone."

Understand that "the zone" is the Holy Grail of athletic performance, the top of the performance heap, the peak athletic experience. The zone is flow; flow is the zone. The terms are interchangeable, and when you get in the zone, you immediately start playing to your full potential in whatever game you are playing. That's what is meant by "the zone". That's what is meant by "flow".

The zone, however, is thought to occur only by chance, not choice.

Sport psychologists agree that the flow state exists, but they insist that you cannot make it happen intentionally. Yet here I was, intentionally doing this imaginary thing on the court that went totally against everything I had ever been taught about how to play tennis properly, and to my complete surprise, every time I did it, I found myself right square in the middle of the zone. And every time I stopped doing it, I went right back to playing "in the norm."

Even my friend noticed the difference and asked me what I was doing, so I showed him and he agreed to give it a try. To our mutual surprise he, too, *immediately* started playing tennis in the zone!

"You've really hit on something here," he said.

I wasn't exactly sure what I'd hit on, but for the next hour we shared an extraordinary human experience; an experience found in all sports, at all skill levels, and in every culture in the world. We shared the peak human experience of playing in the zone.

My own feeling at the time was that I had accidentally stumbled across something huge, a way to immediately access the zone. I vividly remember thinking to myself, "Oh, my God! I found it!" And at that very moment, my life changed. Not because I had tripped over the secret to sport's greatest mystery. That was certainly a part of it, and it has completely changed the way I teach the game of tennis. But the real change came from something far deeper; something that reached all the way down to my very being. It was like a part of me that had been sleeping in the background of my existence was suddenly and abruptly awakened.

Every time I got in the zone, I felt like I was being introduced to a new person, a new me, and I sensed that this new me was the *real me*, the *true me*, the me who had been there all along just waiting to come outside and play. And now that this new me had been awakened, I knew I could never go back. I could never return to my former self, and whenever I came out of the zone, whenever I returned to playing in the norm, I immediately felt incomplete, unfulfilled, as if I had fallen backwards into a perpetual lie. Only now, I know exactly how to return to the truth. After this accidental awakening, two things became apparent.

1. I had to develop my ability to maintain this awakened state – a personal journey that continues to this day.
2. I had to share this incredible experience with others. This was something I could not keep to myself. The way I figured it, if I could wake up, others could too.

As luck would have it, my practice partner that day was a clinical psychologist, and when I asked him to explain the psychology of what had just happened to both of us, he said he wasn't exactly sure, but that he had some books I could read. That day I started reading about higher consciousness and the mind, studying this flow experience from the outside by reading about it, while every day I also spent as much time as possible observing this experience from the inside by playing this new, imaginary game. It seemed perfectly logical to me that the best way to develop my own true nature was to get into the higher conscious state that awakened it, and that meant getting in the zone and experiencing it from the inside.

This "inside – outside" approach to studying the zone and its higher conscious state eventually led me to the works of the integral community, particularly the writings of Ken Wilber and Alfred North Whitehead. After reading everything I could find from the Sport Psychology perspective – the perspective that says you *cannot* intentionally create a flow state – my introduction to the integral perspective was like another awakening altogether. I felt like I had come home. Here was a community that not only talked the talk of higher consciousness, but also walked the walk. Nobody in the integral community was saying you couldn't make the reality of flow happen intentionally. In fact, they were saying just the opposite: that indeed you could train yourself to intentionally enter into a flow state and even learn to maintain flow in your daily life.

Wow! Paydirt!

I'd finally found a community that didn't roll its eyes at the mention of higher-consciousness in sport. So I set out to develop this simple approach to accessing the zone, which, when seen through the lens of sport, is a methodology for immediately accessing your peak performance state, but when seen through the lens of consciousness, is a methodology for immediately accessing your *Authentic Self*. To this day, it works for all sports, all skill levels, and all ages. I call it the *Parallel Mode Process*, and it's so easy a child can do it.

Purpose of the book

The purpose of this book is to show you how to gain immediate access to your peak performance state in your chosen sport, which will give you an immediate taste of what it's like to connect to the unified reality of your sport as well as to your own true nature as a human being. It's a powerful experience, not only because of the obvious benefit of intentionally shifting into your peak performance state – you immediately start to play at a noticeably higher level – but also because of the radically different sense of self that you experience when you're in a flow state – a transcendent, selfless state that is free from the bondage of ego.

The Parallel Mode Process shows you how to create the sensorimotor interface between your operating system and your athletic environment that is causal to the human peak performance state. It shows you how to make the one-to-one connection to your athletic environment that is required to experience the unified reality of your sport. Make that one-to-one connection and you will immediately be awakened to your game's highest potential – as well as your own.

The trick, of course, is learning how to make the one-to-one connection to your athletic environment. How do you do that? How do you connect to the unified reality of your sport? Take *your* chosen sport for example – a reality with which you are familiar. Let's say you've played your sport long enough to know what it's about. You may not be an elite performer in your sport, most people aren't, but you've played it long enough to know what it feels like as an athletic experience. You might even have played your sport long enough to have occasionally experienced "the zone." Those times when everything seems to come together simultaneously, those times when you feel totally absorbed in what you are doing, those times when you play at a level noticeably higher than your norm. You're not sure why it happened; you only know that when it happens, everything seems right, and you want it to continue.

And then it goes away!

Just as mysteriously as it appears and gives you a glimpse of the game's unified reality, it suddenly disappears, leaving you to wonder what the heck just happened and how do you make it happen again?

If you have ever had this experience, if you have ever experienced playing your sport "in the zone," then you have experienced a one-to-one connection to the unified reality of your sport. You have also experienced a one-to-one connection to your own unified reality, the authentic you, the whole you, you functioning at your full potential in the competitive environment of your sport. And the time you spend awakened to this transcendent reality is time spent at your full potential. It's also time spent at the leading edge of your own evolution as a human being.

That's a challenging reality in which to spend your time, and this book is designed to show you how to awaken to this transcendent reality in your sport. In this postmodern world of evolving consciousness, playing in the zone is not only a way of waking up to your full potential as an athlete, it's also a way of waking up to your Authentic Self as a human being.

A Simple Shift

Being able to intentionally create the zone when I played tennis allowed me to experience the zone from inside the experience itself. But it also allowed me to observe what I was doing differently with my operating system that always caused me to get into the zone. By "operating system", I mean the human sensorimotor operating system that continuously interfaces with and within the athletic environment.

Each day, after subjectively experiencing my flow state *from the inside*, I was able to objectively reconstruct what my operating system was doing differently *on the outside*. And what I noticed was that whenever I made a very simple shift in my exterior mode of operation, not only did it cause an immediate and noticeable improvement in my level of play, but this shift in my *exterior mode of operation* was always accompanied by an immediate and noticeable shift in my *interior state of consciousness.*

Always. It never failed. And it never failed when my students made the same shift in their exterior mode of operation. This seemingly causal shift was a shift from playing in a Serial Mode of operation to playing in a Parallel Mode of operation. Immediately upon making this operational shift from Serial Mode to Parallel Mode, players would experience two things:

1. A noticeable improvement in their performance.
2. A noticeable shift in their conscious state.

Always. Skill level didn't seem to matter. From novice to elite, the experience was always the same: players would immediately get in the zone when they made this operational shift from Serial Mode to Parallel

Mode, and as long as they maintained their Parallel Mode of operation, they would also maintain their peak performance state with its higher state of consciousness. But the instant they returned to their normal, Serial Mode of operation, they would also return to their normal performance state and their normal state of consciousness.

More about the differences between Serial Mode and Parallel Mode a little later, but for now, it's only important to understand that making the shift from your Serial Mode of operation to your Parallel Mode of operation is as easy or as hard as you want to make it. Kids have no problem shifting to their Parallel Mode. We adults, on the other hand, are so psychologically conditioned to the state of consciousness that accompanies our Serial Mode of operation that any operational shift that brings with it a change in consciousness will be disconcerting at first. You can count on it.

The saving grace in shifting to your Parallel Mode is that it works a heck of a lot better than your Serial Mode. In fact, your Parallel Mode is the most efficient and accurate way you can use your sensorimotor operating system to connect to and interface with the ongoing action in your athletic environment – whether it's a tennis environment, a baseball/softball environment, soccer, lacrosse, strength training, volleyball, golf, basketball, jogging, or even walking around the block. The environment doesn't matter. Your connection to that environment does.

Performance is not about the environment. It's about how efficiently and how accurately your operating system connects to and interfaces with that environment. And when it comes to the difference between performing in your Serial Mode versus performing in your Parallel Mode, there's no contest. You in your Parallel Mode of operation will perform at a higher level than you in your Serial Mode of operation.

Here's the thing about playing in the zone. You don't play better because you are "in the zone." You play better because when you are in the zone your sensorimotor operating system is functioning in its most efficient and accurate mode of operation – the Parallel Mode.

You can't help but play at a higher level when you shift to your Parallel Mode of operation. It happens all by itself, as if by accident, as if it came over you for no apparent reason – by chance, not by choice.

Except that now you have a choice in the matter. And the choice is to shift from your Serial Mode of operation to your Parallel Mode of operation. Make the intentional shift to your Parallel Mode and you create a simultaneous shift in your conscious state, which brings with it a very different perception of reality.

Making the Shift

How do you make the shift from your Serial Mode of operation to your Parallel Mode of operation? Here's exactly what I did on that summer day in 1978 that caused me to immediately start playing tennis in the zone.

While I was practicing with my psychologist friend, I noticed that I was hitting the ball late, my timing was off, which resulted in me missing shots I knew I should make. It was frustrating to me as a tennis pro, yet I wasn't exactly sure how to fix my timing problem. There was nothing in the sports literature at the time explaining how to correct bad timing, but it was apparent to me that I was hitting the ball late and I needed to fix the problem or my game would continue to frustrate me.

I'm still not sure why I did what I did next because it was so unlike me, so out-of-character, so silly and childlike, and yet it made complete sense to me as a way to fix my timing. What I decided to do was imagine a big picture window spanning the court in front of me where I thought I should contact the ball. It looked like this:

To me, the logic was simple: if I hit the ball at my imaginary window, then the timing of my contact would be good, but if I hit the ball behind my imaginary window, then the timing of my contact would be bad. Simple.

- Contact at my imaginary window – good timing.
- Contact behind my imaginary window – bad timing.

As we hit the ball back and forth across the net and I started noticing more closely the location of my contact - I saw that almost every ball was getting past my imaginary window. I was contacting every ball late relative to the location of my window, and to fix the problem I decided to concentrate on watching the ball more closely. The way I figured it, if I focused on the ball as intently as I could, then I would always make contact at my imaginary window. But that's not what happened. What happened was that I kept making contact behind my imaginary window no matter how closely I focused on the ball. *It was like I knew where the ball was, but I didn't know where my imaginary window was.*

That seemed backwards to me, so I decided to do something completely different. Instead of concentrating on the ball, I decided to concentrate on my imaginary window. I literally visualized this great big window in front of me, which caused me to visually and mentally focus on my window instead of on the ball, and instead of using my racquet to hit the ball back over the net, I decided to use my racquet to keep every ball from getting past my imaginary window.

That was it. That was all I was going to do: use my racquet to keep every ball from getting past my imaginary window.

I didn't care how I did it or what I looked like doing it. As long as I kept the ball from getting past my imaginary window, I knew that whatever my technique looked like, it would be perfectly timed.

I had no idea what would happen when I shifted my focus from the ball to this imaginary window, and I didn't care. My sole objective was to defend my imaginary window with my racquet, and to keep myself on task, I simply said "yes" when I was successful in defending my window and "no" when I wasn't – immediate verbal feedback.

As I started to play this imaginary game of defending my window, I heard myself saying, "yes – no – no – yes." At first, my timing was still erratic, but I stuck with it. It was fun and I found myself becoming more and more absorbed in this childlike game of defending my imaginary window with my racquet.

Then I heard myself saying, "yes – yes – yes - yes," and, suddenly, I was not only keeping every ball from getting past my window, but everything I hit was going back over the net, even though I wasn't consciously *trying* to hit the ball back over the net! All I was conscious of doing was using my racquet to keep every oncoming ball from getting past this big, imaginary window in front of me, and the more I did it, the more I realized that this imaginary game was working a lot better than my normal game!

And as I became more deeply absorbed in playing this imaginary game, it suddenly hit me that I had felt this way before – on those rare occasions when I had, for some unknown reason, played the game of tennis "in the zone." A wave of complete ecstasy washed over me: "Oh my God!" I thought, "I found it!"

At that very moment, I woke up. The *real me* was awakened. I felt whole, complete, one with the game, one with myself, one with everything. I suddenly became aware of my highest level of performance. I knew I was in the zone, and I watched in amazement as every one of my shots went effortlessly back across the net.

And then it went away.

As quickly as this sense of oneness had come over me, it was gone, leaving me back in my normal performance state, missing the same shots I had just been making, feeling frustrated again, completely out of the zone, completely back to normal.

Only this time, I recognized what had caused me to come out of the zone. It happened when I started watching my shots go back over the net. It happened when I stopped focusing on my imaginary window and went back to focusing on the ball, watching my results, getting caught up in how well I was playing, and when I returned to my normal way of focusing – POOF! Just like that, the zone was gone.

So I figured … if it worked once, maybe it would work again, and I immediately stopped focusing on my shots and again started focusing on defending my imaginary window. Sure enough, the same thing happened again, just as suddenly as it had happened before. The moment I stopped focusing on hitting the ball back over the net and started focusing on defending my imaginary window with my racquet, I found myself shifting back into the zone.

I could feel it. I could sense the shift in my performance and in my consciousness, and even though I didn't know what that shift in consciousness was or what it meant, I knew it was required for the shift in my level of performance. Besides, I liked it. It felt right, and I knew, deep down, that this was where I belonged. I had finally come home. This was the real me.

To top it all off, my game was gangbusters! Still not good enough for Wimbledon, but I didn't care! I was playing at my absolute best, and I knew it. I felt it. And I knew something else as well; I knew that this awakening to my full potential was real. There was nothing accidental or artificial about what was happening. I was creating the zone intentionally – by choice, not chance – and it happened to me every time I stopped focusing on the action on the court and started focusing on my imaginary window.

The more I observed what I was doing, the more I realized that it completely defied my Western culture training. I had always been told to "watch the ball," to "focus on the ball," to "concentrate on the ball," but here I was focusing my eyes and my mind on this big imaginary window in front of me, which went totally against everything I had ever learned. I was no longer focusing on the ball; instead I was focusing on the empty space of my *contact zone*. Yet, to my amazement, as I visualized this imaginary window in front of me and kept my focus fixed on my contact zone, I was still able to see all the action on the "other side" of my window. I was literally *focusing on nothing*, but at the same time, I was *seeing everything*! Go figure!

Contact Sequences and Relativity Fields

There are many maps of reality that are meant to better explain human experience, and when I first started investigating the zone as a peak performance experience, I decided to draw a diagram of the basic sequence in tennis; a simple map of the external tennis experience that would allow me to diagram the differences between what I was doing when I was playing in my normal performance state versus what I was doing when I shifted into my peak performance state. It was one map of tennis reality, but it contained two different ways of experiencing that reality.

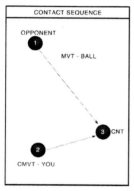

Here's the diagram I drew. I called it a "contact sequence," and it works like this:

First there is the *movement* of the ball (MVT), followed by your *countermovement* to intercept the ball (CMVT), followed by *contact* (CNT), the event that occurs when movement and counter-movement come together at a common point in space and time.

MVT	→	CMVT	→	CNT
1	→	2	→	3

The more I studied this contact sequence pattern, the more I realized it was not only a map of the external reality of tennis; it was also a map of the external reality of every sport involving contact of any kind. This contact sequence map sits at the very bottom of athletic reality. It is a map in which you, as a sensorimotor system of countermovement, are an active participant in the making of the map. Not only are you *in* the map; you are also the *mapmaker*. In other words, in every contact sequence you are a co-creator of your own reality.

What made this map of athletic reality even more interesting was that it was a map of a *complete* contact experience. It had a beginning, middle, and an end; an Alpha Point (the beginning) and an Omega Point (the end), with the Omega Point of the old contact sequence being simultaneously the Alpha Point of the new contact sequence.

Like Whitehead's "actual occasions" (Whitehead 18) this was a complete unit of experience that, at the moment of contact, came to its conclusion as a fully unified field of experience. Every contact sequence also contained what Whitehead calls the "the three notions that complete the Category of the Ultimate." (Whitehead 21) Those notions are: *the one, the many, and creativity.* As you can see, each contact sequence has its own parts (the many), and those parts come together at contact to make a whole (the one), and at contact, something new is always created (creativity).

Cool. The ultimate notions necessary for the creative advance into novelty all right there in this simple map of athletic experience. And what makes it even more interesting is that every contact sequence has both an *absolute nature* as well as a *relative nature.*

The 1→2→3 sequence of MVT→CMVT→CNT is *always* the same. It is always already there in its absolute nature, and that absolute nature *never* changes. But in its relative nature, every contact sequence is *always* changing. No two contact sequences are ever the same, and the fact that every sport involving contact has its own look, its own rules, and its own tools only adds to the relative nature of the contact sequence.

So not only does every contact sequence involve the notions of the ultimate – the one, the many, and creativity – every contact sequence also contains both an absolute nature that never changes *and* a relative nature that is always changing and evolving into something new and different.

But this simple map of the underlying reality of sport also contained something else, a final piece to the puzzle of flow; a piece that was hidden away in the interior logic and structure of every contact sequence.

Here's the contact sequence structure again:

MVT	→	CMVT	→	CNT
1	→	2	→	3
Ball	→	You	→	Contact

Here's the logic: as the system of countermovement in every contact sequence, you, the athlete, are always occupying your *present space*. Physically, you are always "in the present."

MVT	→	CMVT	→	CNT
		(Present)		

Relative to you in the present, movement occurred first, *before countermovement, before the present,* "in the past." So, *relative to you,* movement occurs in the past.

MVT	→	CMVT	→	CNT
(Past)	→	(Present)		

However, relative to both the movement of the ball and your countermovement to intercept the ball, contact occurs last, *after the past and present,* "in the future." So, *relative to movement and countermovement,* contact occurs in the future.

MVT	→	CMVT	→	CNT
(Past)	→	(Present)	→	(Future)

[handwritten: ƠC = obvious]

- First there is movement,
- Then there is countermovement,
- Finally contact.

Here's how every contact sequence looks *in Time:*

MVT	→	CMVT	→	CNT
1	→	2	→	3
Ball	→	You	→	Contact
Past	→	Present	→	Future

But notice the difference in how every contact sequence looks *in Space:*

MVT	→	CNT	←	CMVT
1	→	3	←	2
Ball	→	Contact	←	You
Past	→	Future	←	Present

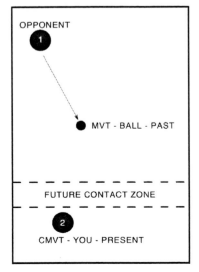

OPPONENT
1

MVT - BALL - PAST

FUTURE CONTACT ZONE

2
CMVT - YOU - PRESENT

And finally, here's how every contact sequence looks in the spatiotemporal reality of tennis or baseball, or any other sport that involves you contacting movement of any kind.

What this map of athletic reality shows is that every contact sequence contains its own interior spatiotemporal reality along with its own absolute and relative nature as well as reality's ultimate categories – the many, the one, and creativity.

That's a lot of stuff going on in one map, but what made this map so valuable to my own investigation of the zone was that it showed the difference between what I was focusing on when I focused on the ball versus what I was focusing on when I focused on my imaginary window.

What I realized was that when I focused on the ball, I was focusing on the past relative to me in the present. So while my body was physically in the present, *my mind was focused on the past.* Granted, it was the immediate past, but the past nonetheless. The logical conclusion was that when I was playing in my normal performance state, focusing on the ball, on form, on the objects of the material dimension of the contact sequence, I was playing *"in the past."*

The human peak performance state is definitely *not* about playing in the past. One of the major characteristics of flow reported by athletes from around the world is the sense of being *"in the present."* Anyone who has ever been in the zone knows the feeling of total presence, the sense of being one with the game, one with everything, one with the flow of the action. That's exactly how I felt every time I started defending my imaginary window with my racquet. And as I looked at what was actually happening according to this map of the temporal and spatial reality of sport, I saw the hidden piece to the puzzle of flow.

What I realized was that as I was visualizing this imaginary window in front of me, I was no longer focusing on the ball, no longer focusing on the past. Instead, I was focusing on my contact zone, focusing on the *future depth of contact* while, at the same time, I was observing the *past movement of the ball.* In other words, *I was focused on the future while simultaneously seeing the past, which meant that I was aware of the past and the future equally and simultaneously.*

My eyes were inputting *parallel streams* of visual information to my brain about the past and the future of the arising contact sequence, and those parallel streams of past and future combined to co-create the spatiotemporal dimension of the *present.*

With that realization, I had another awakening. Everything about playing in the zone started to make sense – right then, right there. The underlying spatiotemporal dimension of flow is the dimension of the present, and by inputting parallel streams of visual information about the past and the future equally and simultaneously, the human operating system actively co-creates a *nondual interface* with the past and future dimensions of its arising contact sequence pattern. A nondual interface in which the past and the future are no longer separate dimensions. The past and the future are no longer two, but rather they combine to co-create the unified spatiotemporal reality of the present dimension. And with the co-creation of the present dimension comes the co-creation of the underlying spatiotemporal dimension of flow.

This simple map of the contact sequence turned out to be a map of much more than just swatting a tennis ball or hitting a baseball, of kicking soccer balls, or spiking volleyballs. It was a map of the spatial and temporal relativity of a single athletic moment, a droplet of athletic experience in Space and Time, a moment in which the parts come together to create a unified whole. This simple little diagram was a map of *a unified temporal and spatial relativity field.*

Wow! The map I started out with had certainly come a long way! Just as my ability to get into and maintain the zone had evolved, so, too, had my understanding of this map of reality. It was no longer just a map of a single contact sequence. It was now a map of a single *Relativity Field.*

I called them *R-Fields* for short, and every time your countermovement comes together with the movement of any object in your athletic environment, you create a contact event that turns this R-field into a unified whole, and at that very moment of conclusion comes the creation of a new and different R-field. Or, as Whitehead put it: *"The many become one and are increased by one."* (Whitehead 21)

Two Visual Strategies

A little bit of basic science here – and I do mean basic! In fast-moving ball sports such as tennis or baseball, volleyball, or lacrosse, your sensorimotor operating system functions as an *Input-Processing-Output* system that connects to and interfaces with the moment-to-moment action of your sport. To interface with this action, your eyes must input visual information to your brain about the action in your visual field. In ball sports this means visual information about the movement of the ball, your opponent's movements, the location of your target, etc. Your brain then processes and integrates that visual information and outputs relative motor information to your body, which in turn creates a countermovement that directly relates to the movement of the ball.

The more accurate your visual input, the more accurate your motor output, and the more accurate your motor output, the more accurately your countermovements relate to the movement of the ball. Add all this accuracy together and you get an accurate contact event. You get *Positive Contact*. Likewise, inaccurate visual input produces inaccurate motor output, which, in turn, produces an inaccurate contact event: *Negative Contact*.

This is basic stimulus-response with the end result being either an event of positive or negative contact. In any sport, the one thing you do not want to do is create negative contact. Negative contact always loses. Positive contact, on the other hand, gives you a chance to win. The point is that in order to create positive contact, your eyes must input accurate visual information to your brain about the action occurring in your visual R-field environment.

When I grew up playing tennis and baseball, football, and basketball, we were all taught to use our eyes one way and one way only. We

> USEFUL – NOT GARBAGE
> NOT IRRELEVANT

were taught to "watch the ball," to "focus on the ball," to "concentrate on the ball." That was it. That was how you did it. There was nothing in the athletic coaching community that spoke to alternative visual input strategies.

But the more I studied the zone from inside the experience, the more I realized that I was using my eyes in a completely different way. I was using a completely different *visual input strategy*. I was no longer watching the ball in the traditionally accepted way. Instead, I was using my eyes in a radically different way, and I started explaining the difference between these two visual strategies using this simple visual analogy.

Imagine standing behind a big glass window, watching as a boy throws a snowball at your window.

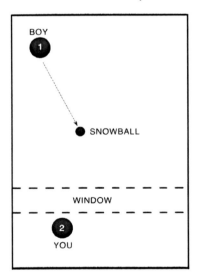

Now imagine that your visual objective is to have the "SPLAT" of the snowball against your window clearly in focus exactly *when* and *where* it happens. Logically, if you have the splat clearly in focus when and where it happens, then you have located the contact point along the surface of your window.

This visual objective is the same as your visual objective in any fast-moving ball sport where you have to locate a contact point along the flight line of the ball. Hitting a tennis ball or a baseball, catching a football, kicking a soccer ball; these are all athletic challenges in which the creation of positive contact requires you to input accurate visual information to your brain about a *positive contact point* located somewhere along the flight line of the ball.

Using this snowball/window analogy, you can see how it is possible to use your eyes in two completely different ways to achieve the same

But You can't [illegible] the Ball [illegible] the 60 - 60.

visual objective, which is to locate the contact point – the SPLAT – exactly when and where it happens on your window.

The first method is to keep the snowball in focus along its flight line from start to finish, from the point the boy throws the snowball to the point it splats against your window. Logically, if you keep the snowball in focus all the way to your window, you will have the splat clearly in focus exactly when and where it happens, successfully achieving your visual objective.

When I first started studying visual strategies, I sought the help of Dr. William Hines, who, at the time, was Team Ophthalmologist for the Denver Broncos and Colorado Avalanche and one of the world's leading authorities on sports vision. He suggested that I call this first visual strategy a "Variable-Depth of Focus Visual Input Pattern" or VDF for short. Simply put, VDF requires you to refocus your eyes from one depth to another in order to keep the ball in focus along its flight line from start to finish, thus the term "Variable-Depth of Focus."

VDF is the traditionally accepted strategy for using your eyes in any fast-moving ball sport. VDF is "watching the ball," and because you have to refocus your eyes sequentially from one fixation point to another in order to keep the ball in focus from start to finish, VDF is inherently a *Serial Input Pattern* (that is, information is processed sequentially, one fixation point at a time).

The second visual strategy you can use to locate the splat of the snowball on your window we called a "Fixed-Depth of Focus Visual Input Pattern" or FDF for short. FDF requires you to keep your eyes focused on your window and simply look along the surface of the window for the point the snowball splats against the window. *Focus on your window, look for the splat.* It's really very easy.

And here's the best part. Since your window is already in focus as the snowball approaches, not only will you "see" the snowball come into focus as it gets closer to your window, but since your eyes are already *prefocused* on the depth of contact, the splat of the snowball on window will be clearly in focus exactly when and where it happens, thus achieving your visual objective. Only this time, you achieved your visual objective without having to refocus your eyes. *Prefocusing eliminates refocusing*, which makes FDF a much more efficient way to locate the splat on your window.

But the biggest difference between variable depth of focus and fixed depth of focus is that with a fixed depth of focus input pattern not only are you able to see the snowball *and* your window at the same time, you are also inputting parallel streams of visual information to your brain about the location of the snowball *and* the location of your contact zone. Thus fixed depth of focus is inherently a *Parallel Input Pattern* (that is, multiple pieces of information are processed simultaneously).

Serial Input (VDF) = watch the ball from release point to contact point.

Parallel Input (FDF) = focus on your window, look for the contact point.

What struck me as important about these two completely different ways of using your eyes was that *everyone* has the ability to use their eyes in either a Serial Input Pattern (VDF) or a Parallel Input Pattern (FDF). It's actually a choice you can make, and when you choose to use your eyes in a Serial Input Pattern, you are also choosing a Serial Mode as your overall mode of operation.

Serial Input → Serial Processing → Serial Output = *Serial Mode of Operation*

But if you choose to use your eyes in a Parallel Input Pattern, you are also choosing a Parallel Mode as your overall mode of operation.

Parallel Input → Parallel Processing →   Parallel Output =
                                         Parallel Mode of Operation

It all boils down to how your eyes organize the information available to you in your visual R-field environment. Every R-field contains information about the *past* as well as information about the *future*, information about *form* as well as information about the *empty space of your contact zone*. How much of that information you choose to make available to your brain is up to you, but if you want to experience your full potential as an athlete, then your best bet is to allow your operating system to interface with the full potential of your athletic environment. And that means shifting your operating system from its Serial Mode to its Parallel Mode.

How? By fixing the focus of your eyes on the empty space of your contact zone and letting form arise in its moment-to-moment manifestation.

Sounds easy, doesn't it?

In theory, it is. Shift into your Parallel Mode and you shift into the zone. In practice, however, making the shift to your Parallel Mode is a challenging proposition. Yet it is a challenge we must all face if we want to experience a flow state. When you break it down, the challenge of playing in the zone comes in two parts: an exterior part that is visible and manifests as peak performance, and an interior part that is invisible and manifests as a higher state of consciousness. Every athlete I have worked with over the years gets very excited about the exterior part – the peak performance part. Unfortunately, not every athlete gets excited about the interior part – the higher consciousness part.

Therein lies the rub. You can't have one without the other. You can't have peak performance without a higher state of consciousness, nor can you have a higher state of consciousness without peak performance, which means that if you want to play your chosen sport in the zone, then you have to be willing to make a shift not only in your exterior mode of operation, but also in your interior state of consciousness.

That's the challenge of the zone. *Inside and outside, you have to change everything.*

Some athletes are not willing to make these changes. The shift to a Parallel Mode requires more of them than they are willing to give. Any change that takes them out of the comfort zone of their normal state of consciousness is too radical, too different. The exterior payoff is not worth the interior cost. So be it. That's their choice.

Others, however, are willing to make the necessary changes in both their exterior mode of operation and their interior state of consciousness. They are not only aware of the higher level of performance they get when they shift to their Parallel Mode, they are also aware of the change in conscious states that accompanies their Parallel Mode. This change in conscious states might be experienced as a deeper level of concentration, or it might be experienced as a heightened awareness of their environment. They might feel a sense of being fully present to the action on the court or the field of competition, but whatever their perception of this different state of consciousness, they realize that it is part and parcel of their flow experience. Without this higher state of consciousness there would be no flow.

These are the athletes who are awakening to their own full potential. For them, it's not only about performing at a higher level, it's also about maintaining this new and very different interior state known as "unity" or "integral" consciousness, and the more these athletes choose to intentionally create and maintain their Parallel Mode of operation with its integral state of consciousness, the more they are awakened to their own true nature as human beings.

So there are two sides to the human peak performance experience, and these two sides have very different manifestations. On the exterior side of the experience you can count on immediately performing at a higher level because of the increased efficiency and accuracy of your Parallel Mode of operation. While on the interior side of the experience you can count on something very different indeed. You can count on getting a taste of who you really are; a glimpse of your Authentic Self.

Stick them together and you create the human experience of flow; you at your full potential, interfacing with and within the full potential of your athletic R-field environment.

And you do it by choice, not by chance.

The Full Potential Party

When I was first awakening to my own flow state, I knew deep down that in order to become more familiar with this radically different reality, I had to become more familiar with focusing on the empty space of my contact zone while the action in my visual field arose in its moment-to-moment advance. The ability to maintain focus on my contact zone, however, did not come overnight, nor did it come without some major changes in my overall sense of self.

As I practiced shifting out of a VDF input pattern and shifting into a FDF input pattern, I found myself detaching my focus from the people, places and objects in my visual field, and as I stopped focusing on the individual pieces of the action in front of me, something extraordinary happened: *I started seeing all of the pieces simultaneously.*

It felt like a new and different reality was introducing itself to me. A reality that I would later come to understand had always been there; a reality that was all around me, but because of the way I was using my eyes to focus sequentially on the different objects in my visual field, because of the way I was visually differentiating this ever-present reality, I had never come to know its unified, undifferentiated oneness, the ever-present oneness that is always there for each of us to experience.

The only times I had ever glimpsed this oneness had been on those rare occasions when I had accidentally shifted into the zone. Only now, I was shifting into the zone intentionally by shifting my visual focus from VDF to FDF, and the practice of fixing my focus on the empty space of my contact zone immediately stopped the visual differentiation that had been such a part of my variable focus performance state. Best of all, as I continued to develop my ability to maintain a fixed focus when I played, I continued to develop an ever-expanding awareness of this unified reality that was opening up to me on a daily basis.

At first, this shift to FDF was confusing and difficult to maintain simply because I wasn't sure what would happen when I stopped focusing on the individual parts of the game, particularly when I stopped focusing on the ball. It was like letting go of the one object that had always anchored me to what I thought was the reality of the game. Learning to focus on my contact zone meant learning to accept what was happening in my visual field without identifying with any of it. Whenever I would return to focusing on the ball or any other part of the action, I would find myself coming out of the zone and immediately identifying with the part of the action on which I was focused. For example, if I focused again on the ball, I would immediately start making judgments about its speed, spin, angle, and bounce. *That's what I was taught to do.* That was the only way to focus, the only rational way to use my eyes.

But here I was, doing something seemingly *irrational*, exactly the opposite of what I had been taught to do. I was intentionally *defocusing* from the action in my visual field by focusing on my contact zone, and it didn't take long to realize that when I stopped focusing on the ball, or the player, or the court and started focusing on my contact zone, I also stopped identifying with the individual objects in my visual field, even though I was still aware of them all. And when I stopped identifying with the people, places, and objects in my visual field, I also stopped judging them. I was finding this experience of playing in the zone to be an experience of awareness without judgment, awareness without attachment, awareness without the constant approvals and disapprovals that were such a part of my normal performance state.

It all seemed very strange at first, like I wasn't doing everything I was supposed to be doing; like I wasn't thinking about everything I was supposed to be thinking about. I wasn't focusing on all the things I was supposed to be focused on. The game wasn't supposed to be this easy. It wasn't supposed to be this fluid, this free from the incessant chattering in my head. And yet, whenever I shifted into the zone, there was always one characteristic that I could not deny. I knew for certain that I was performing at my highest level. That part was obvious to me as a professional athlete. Physically, I couldn't lie to myself about how well I was playing. I couldn't fake my own full potential.

At the same time, there was more to this full potential experience than just the physical part. The more I practiced creating and maintaining the zone, the more I realized that there were other parts of me being awakened at the same time. Maintaining a Parallel Mode exterior was opening up interior experiences that were very new to me and very different from my norm. What I was learning about the zone was that it included not only significant differences in my physical experiences of the game; it also included significant differences in my emotional, mental, and spiritual experiences, and if I wanted to stay in the zone, I couldn't side-step any of these interior differences. They were *always* there, and it became increasingly apparent to me that in order to develop this Parallel Mode exterior, I would have to simultaneously develop its correlative interior and the very different emotional, mental, and spiritual states that always accompanied this newly awakened state of integral consciousness.

I'd heard of people having "white-light" experiences in which they became suddenly and fully enlightened, but that was not the way this process worked for me. No white lights, no magical enlightenment, nothing but an accidental awakening to this extraordinary experience of playing in the zone followed by a dogged willingness to undergo the day-to-day practice of a process that brought with it a radically different sense of who I was, or, more exactly, who I could become if I chose to walk this path that had evidently been there all along. I just hadn't opened my eyes in a way that made the path visible.

What I found exciting was the fact that I could actually *choose* to walk this different path. I could choose to experience this brand new territory of my Authentic Self. But in order to experience this new and different territory, I had to leave behind the familiar turf of my old self, my old way of playing and the comfort zone of my normal performance state. In one sense, it was exciting. In another sense, it was downright scary! I felt like the proverbial stranger in a strange land. Yet there was one thing about this strange new territory that kept me coming back again and again; one undeniable aspect of playing in the zone that drew me back like a relentless magnet pulling at my soul - and that undeniable aspect was simply this: *it worked better.* Playing in the zone worked better than playing in the norm.

Not only did it work better for me, it also worked better for my students. The same thing that was happening to me was happening to them, and the same choices I had to make had to be made by them. Just as I was being awakened to the full potential of my own flow state by choosing this different path, my students were also being awakened to the full potential of their flow state, and they, too, had to make a choice as to which path they would walk: the old path of normalcy brought on by a Serial Mode of operation, or this new path of interior and exterior awakening brought on by a Parallel Mode of operation. For me, it felt like an invitation to a very special party; the party of my own full potential, and all I had to do was show up.

That's the best thing about human full potential. Everyone is invited. There is no prejudice, no racism, no sexism, no bias, and no bigotry. Full potential is non-exclusionary. I've got mine, you've got yours, and when you come to the full potential party, you find out something very basic about your peak performance state: *it always works better than your normal performance state!*

You play better, you perform at your highest level, and that full potential exterior experience includes a full potential interior experience as well – emotional, mental, and spiritual. Full potential is just that – all-inclusive, fully-integrated; a transcendent experience with one requirement that cannot be overlooked. Like all those who have ventured before us into this vast territory of higher consciousness and human potential, we all step into this territory by ourselves. In the end, we're all required to come to this party alone.

And that takes courage.

The Structure of Performance

A major resource in my study of higher consciousness has been the body of work by Ken Wilber, one of the most influential philosophers and thinkers of our time. Wilber's AQAL (All Quadrants - All Levels - All Lines - All States - All Types) map of reality (another map!) divides all human experience into four different perspectives. Each of these perspectives can be seen in our athletic experiences as well. Here's a quick run-down of the Wilber's AQAL framework as it pertains to sport in general.

- The Upper-Left Quadrant. The Individual-Interior or "I" perspective that is intentional and subjective. My thoughts, feelings, values, motivations; the state of consciousness in which I play my sport.
- The Upper-Right Quadrant. The Individual-Exterior or "It" perspective that is behavioral and objective. My physical body, its biology, neurology, biomechanics; the mode of operation in which I play my sport.
- The Lower-Left Quadrant. The Collective-Interior or "We" perspective that is cultural and intersubjective. The values, language, and mutual understanding and relationships I share with others in the competitive culture of our sport.
- The Lower-Right Quadrant. The Collective-Exterior or "Its" perspective that is social and interobjective. The rules and tools of the particular sport; the athletic environment, its population of players.

INDIVIDUAL INTERIOR Subjective **(Intentional)** "I" Thoughts Feelings Intentions **(Conscious States)**	INDIVIDUAL EXTERIOR Objective **(Behavioral)** "It" Physiology Biology Neurology **(Operating Modes)**
COLLECTIVE INTERIOR Inter Subjective **(Cultural)** "We" Shared Meaning Mutual Understanding Relationships **(Competition)**	**COLLECTIVE EXTERIOR** Inter Subjective **(Social)** "Its" Rules and Tools Population Governance **(Athletic Environment)**

Applying Wilber's AQAL model to sport, we can see that our individual performance experiences, both normal and peak, involve a relationship between interior consciousness (Upper Left quadrant), exterior operation (Upper Right quadrant), the shared interior meaning of our sport (Lower Left quadrant), and the rules and tools of the sport's exterior environment (Lower Right quadrant).

Every time we step into the environment of competition, these four perspectives are always present, providing us with an underlying *structure of performance*. But, as you will see, the underlying structure of our peak performance state is dramatically different from the underlying structure of our normal performance state. Our different performance experiences have different foundational structures, different interior and exterior correlates that co-create the performance experience itself.

For example: we're all familiar with our normal performance state and the normal state of consciousness that accompanies it. This normal state of consciousness is known as *Gross Consciousness*, and this gross interior state has a corresponding exterior correlate – a Serial Mode of operation, which is also our normal mode of operation whether we're playing baseball, basketball, football, tennis, hockey, or jogging in the park.

Our normal performance state has a foundational performance structure that looks like this in the Upper Left and Upper Right quadrants:

NORMAL PERFORMANCE STATE

Gross Conscious State	Serial Operating Mode

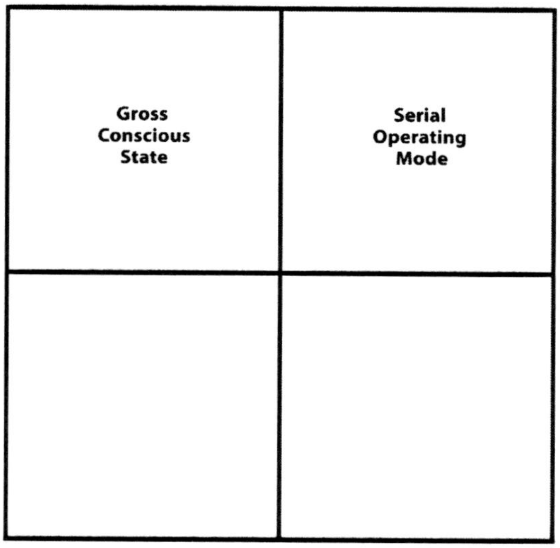

Upper Left   Upper Right

Gross/Interior   ←→   Serial/Exterior

Our peak performance state also has a foundational structure, but it involves a completely different interior state of consciousness – the aforementioned state of integral consciousness, along with a completely different exterior correlate, a Parallel Mode of operation, which is our most efficient and accurate mode of sensorimotor operation.

In short, the performance structure of our peak performance state is radically different from the performance structure of our normal performance state. In the Upper Left and Upper Right quadrants, our peak performance structure looks like this:

PEAK PERFORMANCE STATE

Integral Conscious State	**Parallel Operating Mode**

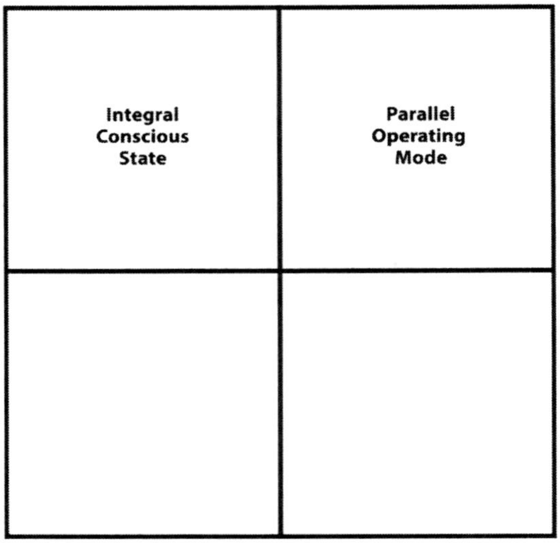

Upper Left Upper Right

Integral/Interior ← →Parallel/Exterior

The simultaneity of these interior and exterior correlates means that if we create one correlate we simultaneously create the other, and that gives us two very different options for creating our peak performance state:

- Option #1: We can create its interior state – a state of integral consciousness – and, in so doing, simultaneously create its exterior correlate – a Parallel Mode of operation.

Or

- Option #2: We can create its exterior mode of operation – a Parallel Mode – and, in so doing, simultaneously create its interior correlate – a state of integral consciousness.

In the summer of 1978, without knowing it, I accidentally stumbled across Option #2.

The imaginary game I started playing in which I used my tennis racquet to keep every ball from getting past my imaginary window was, in fact, a game that caused me to shift out of a Serial Mode of operation and into a Parallel Mode of operation – the exterior mode of operation whose simultaneous interior correlate is a state of integral consciousness.

In other words, I accidentally stumbled across this:

PEAK PERFORMANCE STATE

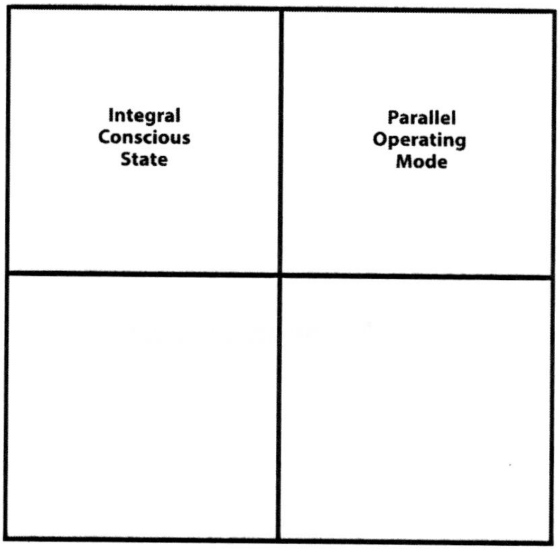

Integral Conscious State	Parallel Operating Mode

Upper Left   Upper Right
Integral/Interior ←→ Parallel/Exterior

When I stopped using my racquet to hit every ball over the net and started using my racquet to prevent every ball from getting past my imaginary window, I was *intentionally* creating the performance structure seen in Option #2. I was intentionally creating the specific *exterior* state of peak performance – a Parallel Mode of operation – and, in so doing; I was simultaneously creating its *interior* correlate – a state of integral consciousness.

End result: immediate access to the unified reality of the human peak performance state; the unified reality of flow.

This is fantastic news for athletes, no matter what your skill level and no matter what your sport. What it means is that you can get in the zone in two entirely different ways. You can create the zone's *interior half* – a state of integral consciousness – and, in so doing, simultaneously create its exterior correlate – a Parallel Mode of operation. Or, you can do it the other way around. You can create the zone's *exterior half* – a Parallel Mode of operation – and, in so doing, simultaneously create its interior correlate – a state of integral consciousness.

Either way, the end result is the same – *the intentional creation of your peak performance state*. Both approaches work, but there is one *huge* difference between these two approaches. With the interior approach, even a glimpse of the zone's unified reality might take years of meditation and mental discipline. The exterior approach, on the other hand, takes only a few minutes.

Let me repeat that. The exterior approach provides *immediate access* to the unified reality of your peak performance state; immediate access to flow. It happens as soon as you shift from your Serial Mode of operation to your Parallel Mode, and learning how to make the shift to your Parallel Mode of operation takes only a few minutes.

But there's a caveat. Even though learning to make the exterior shift to your Parallel Mode takes only a few minutes, this shift in your exterior mode of operation brings with it a corresponding shift in your interior state of consciousness – a shift from gross to integral consciousness – and awakening to the physical, emotional, mental, and spiritual territory of integral consciousness is awakening to the territory of your Authentic Self.

Nurturing and developing *that* territory is a life-long adventure!

Bottom line – you can create the interior state of integral consciousness by intentionally creating its exterior correlate: a Parallel Mode of operation. Think of it as accessing flow through an outside entrance, an exterior doorway to unified reality that you open with your eyes. But in order to open this exterior doorway to the zone, you have to open your eyes in a very different way. You have to open them to the empty space of your contact zone and let form arise in its parade of moment-to-moment presence. With that visual shift, the doorway to the unified reality immediately opens and what you find on the other side will rock your performance world.

The Argument of Sport Psychology

Operationally, getting in the zone comes down to making the shift from a Serial to a Parallel Mode of operation, and making the shift to a Parallel Mode comes down to shifting the way you focus your eyes in your athletic environment. It's the shift from a Variable-Focus State – focusing on form – to a Fixed-Focus State – focusing on empty space - your contact zone – while still "seeing" form.

Could it be that simple? It doesn't seem possible that a shift in the way you focus your eyes could be causal to playing in the zone. Could defocusing from the action in your athletic environment and fixing your focus on the empty space of your contact zone be all it takes to gain immediate access to the unified reality of flow? How could defocusing from form and focusing on empty space create such a major shift in your level of performance as well as in your perception of the game? If it was that easy, then why haven't the sport psychologists of the world already figured this out? With the flow experience being the ultimate experience in sport, you'd think Sport Psychology, as a profession, would have figured it out by now.

Here's the simple truth: it hasn't. The conventional wisdom of Sport Psychology insists that athletes cannot create a flow state by choice. Susan Jackson suggests in her book *Flow in Sports: The Keys to Optimal Experiences and Performances,* that flow "is not a state of mind that can be manufactured and distributed in packaged form." (Jackson 161) At best, athletes can only prepare for flow by bringing together the various mental, physical, emotional, and spiritual components of flow – 9 or 10 at last count – and then hope for flow to happen.

Good luck with that!

The most convincing argument Sport Psychology gives for an

athlete's inability to intentionally create flow is that one of these flow components is a *loss of self-consciousness*. In other words, flow is an unselfconscious state – a selfless state – and, according to Sport Psychology, a selfless state cannot be created through self-will, which means you can't get in the zone on purpose. End of story. So say the experts in the field.

With all due respect to the experts, that's not the end of the story by any means. Yes, it's a logical argument, but it's also the argument that keeps Sport Psychology locked inside its box of partially effective interventions. It's one thing to *prepare* for flow through relaxation techniques, imagery rehearsal, mind-set training, and a host of well-intentioned psychological interventions, but it's quite another to *make flow happen on purpose*. The real question is not "what can we do to better prepare for flow," but rather, "what can we do to intentionally create a flow state?" If flow is the *effect*, then what is the *cause*?

Integral theory allows us to look for the cause from the exterior perspective of system dynamics rather than limiting the search to the interior, mental perspective taken by Sport Psychology, and it is through this exterior perspective of system dynamics that the Parallel Mode Process teaches athletes how to intentionally create the unified reality of flow. Think of it this way: your Parallel Mode of operation with its corresponding state of integral consciousness is the *cause*. Flow is the *effect*.

CAUSE		EFFECT
Integral/Interior ← → Parallel Mode/Exterior		Flow/Zone

Create the structure that simultaneously creates flow's causal spatio-temporal dimension – the flowing present – and the effect you produce is the flow state. Maintain that structure throughout your performance and you will maintain a flow state as well. In other words: maintain your Parallel Mode of operation and you maintain flow.

So while Sport Psychology sticks to its guns and insists that you cannot create a selfless state through self-will, the Parallel Mode Process suggests that, in fact, you can use your self-will to intentionally create the spatiotemporal interface that is causal to the flow state, and with the creation of a flow state comes a loss of self-consciousness. End result: a selfless state. And you did it through your own self-will!

ۑ

An Outside Entrance

Part of what makes your peak performance state so challenging is that it *does* involve a selfless state, meaning you have to be willing to let go of your ordinary sense of self in order to maintain flow's interior state of integral consciousness. That's the *interior perspective* taken by Sport Psychology as well as the Eastern Wisdom Traditions. In 1974, Timothy Gallwey brought the interior practices of Zen into the Western world of tennis with his highly successful *Inner Game of Tennis*. "Self 1" (the teller) and "Self 2" (the doer) became terms of art in this newly emerging "inner" approach to the game; the idea being to get Self 1, the teller, out of the way so that Self 2, the doer, could play the game without any interference from Self 1. An amazingly simple approach to playing the game, and it worked!

But in 1974, there were many in the tennis teaching profession, myself included, who thought the Zen approach was an easy out for teachers who could neither play the game nor teach the game. The only rational way to play the game and teach the game was through the development of sound biomechanical techniques, while "mental toughness" was gained through years of hard work and practice. That was me in 1974.

A few years later, after my accidental awakening to the zone, I didn't think the interior approach was so crazy after all, but I came to that realization from the opposite direction – from the chance discovery of an exterior mode of operation that produced the same interior state of consciousness as Gallwey's Zen approach. But I also found that the process I was developing had its own version of Self 1 and Self 2, and it came in the form of Serial and Parallel Modes of operation. In a Serial Mode, Self 1, the teller, was always present, jabbering away as I played.

In a Parallel Mode, however, Self 1 disappeared and the doer, Self 2, was left alone to play the game without the boundaries imposed by Self 1 and its Serial Mode of operation.

Again, the shift in interior consciousness was being produced by a shift in exterior operation. It was like I had chanced upon an outer entrance to the inner game, and in order to make that inner shift to integral consciousness, all I had to do was make the outer shift to a Parallel Mode of operation. And in order to shift into a Parallel Mode of operation, all I had to do was shift the way I was using my visual focus from VDF, the input pattern of the teller, to FDF, the input pattern of the doer. In other words, I had to get VDF out of the way so that FDF could be my input pattern without any interference from VDF.

When seen from this *exterior perspective*, the perspective of visual system dynamics, you still have to be willing to let go of something, but in this exterior, Upper-Right quadrant perspective, you have to be willing to let go of the way you normally use your eyes. You have to be willing to defocus from the people, places, and objects in your visual field and focus instead on your contact zone. You have to stop focusing on form (VDF) and start focusing on the empty space of your contact zone (FDF).

From the Upper-Left quadrant's interior perspective, every bit of this has to do with detaching from self, and detaching from self is confusing, to say the least. Anything that deals with the interior perspective is inherently confusing. When we start delving into our thoughts, our emotions, our feelings, our values and intentions, we start delving into ambiguous territory. The interior dimension of athletic experience is not easily explained, and one of the most difficult aspects to explain is the loss of self-consciousness that *must* occur if we are to experience flow.

Fortunately, the selfless interior of flow has an exterior correlate, and that exterior correlate is a Parallel Mode of operation brought about by fixing your focus on the empty space of your contact zone

$F = fixed$

$V = VARIABLE$

while simultaneously "seeing" the action as it arises in its moment-to-moment procession. To use our window analogy, you create a Parallel Mode of operation by fixing your focus on your window while simultaneously seeing the action as it arises on the other side of your window.

In essence, you are focused on the whole environment while simultaneously seeing its parts, and *that's* how you create a unified interface with any athletic environment. *You do it by interfacing with both form and empty space, equally and simultaneously,* and by creating this unified *exterior* interface, you simultaneously create its unified *interior* correlate of integral consciousness, and it is the simultaneity of this unified interior-exterior structure that acts to co-create the experience of flow; a fully-unified state of being that includes as one of its characteristics, a loss of self-consciousness.

That's how you do it. That's how you create a selfless state through self-will. You just go about it from the outside instead of from the inside.

DEPTH of Focus

Fighting the Battle

Creating the zone is easy with this uniquely different process. *Maintaining* the zone, however, is the battle you must fight. To create the zone, all you have to do is shift into a Parallel Mode and you immediately create the simultaneous connection to form an empty space that is the zone's unified interface. End result: immediate access to the unified reality of flow. That's the easy part. The hard part, the battle, comes when you start trying to maintain the zone's unified interface during competition. That's when ego starts hammering on you to stop with all this craziness and return to your comfort zone. Stop focusing on nothing and get back to where you belong – focusing on everything! There's the battle you will fight, and it's a very real battle.

I found myself fighting this battle each and every day as I tried to stay focused on my contact zone in the midst of all the action. And it was a hard-fought battle. Every part of me said focusing on my contact zone was wrong. It felt completely backwards, but the more I practiced defocusing from the action on the court and keeping my focus fixed on my contact zone, the more I sensed myself winning the battle. And the only reason I kept fighting the battle was that whenever I maintained a fixed-focus on my contact zone, I always found myself playing in the zone. Always.

The same thing happened with my students. Every time they maintained a fixed-focus on their contact zone, they, too, found themselves playing in the zone. But they also found themselves fighting the same battle: the battle to remain focused on their contact zone (empty space) and defocused from the ball or their opponent (form). Quite frankly, some were willing to fight the battle; some were not, even if it meant no longer accessing their peak performance state.

"It's too hard," they said. "I can't do it," they said. "I can't focus on nothing!"

Well, in fact, they could, but they chose not to. And I understood that choice. To this day, I still understand that choice simply because it is hard to focus on nothing. Focusing on empty space requires total concentration, total control of your visual and mental focus; total absorption on the task of focusing on your contact zone. *But that's the whole point!* One of the primary characteristics of the zone, as described by athletes of every sport from every corner of the world, is that the zone is a state of total concentration, total focus.

From Susan Jackson's *Flow in Sports: The Keys to Optimal Experiences and Performances:*

> *Focus in flow is complete and purposeful, with no extraneous thoughts distracting from the task at hand...In flow there is no room for any thoughts other than what you are doing and feeling right at the moment, the now. Concentration is a critical component and one of the characteristics of optimal experience mentioned most often. (Jackson 25)*

Focus is "complete and purposeful," which is exactly what it takes to maintain a fixed-focus on your contact zone, no matter what your sport. Think about it. It takes complete control of your visual and mental focus to keep your eyes focused on your contact zone while witnessing all the action taking place in your visual field. That's the battle you will face. You can't avoid it. It is a battle for control of your focus; either *you* control your focus and put it exactly where it will do you the most good – on your contact zone – or you let your focus be controlled by the action in your visual field. This battle to control your focus is the exterior correlate to the interior battle to detach from the self-conscious limitations that inhibit your performance. The Parallel Mode Process suggests that you fight this interior battle to detach from self by fighting its exterior correlate – the battle to defocus from form.

In other words, by fixing your focus on the empty space of your contact zone, you simultaneously defocus from the people, places, and objects to which "self" attaches. Focusing on your contact zone is focusing on nothing, "no-thing." Self is thus attached to nothing. So instead of self relative to the people, places, and objects of form, you have created an experience of self relative to empty space, self relative to nothing. And self relative to nothing is "no self;" the selfless state in which you are released from the bondage of ego and invited to experience the freedom and fullness of your own true nature.

With the Parallel Mode Process, you win the interior battle of detaching from self by winning the exterior battle of defocusing from form.

Focus and Attachment

When we focus our eyes on something in our visual field, we automatically attach to that "something." Our minds attach to what we focus on with our eyes, and in fast-moving contact sports such as baseball or tennis, softball or soccer, the fact that we are taught from day one to focus on the ball, means that not only are we taught to focus our *eyes* on the ball, we are also taught to focus our *minds* on the ball, which is exactly the reason we normally play these sports in a Serial Mode of operation with its gross conscious state. By visually attaching to the various parts of the action, we literally lock ourselves into a Serial Mode of operation. This Serial Mode of visually and mentally attaching to the action seems completely logical because it allows us to make sense out of the fast-moving world of our athletic environment.

Serial visual input allows us to differentiate the parts of our visual environment that are important to our task from those that are unimportant. Those parts we deem unimportant are left in the background, out of focus. We still see them peripherally, but because we remain defocused from them, we assign them no value. What we value most in these fast-moving environments is usually the object of contact, so, quite naturally, we focus on the object of contact with our eyes. We visually attach to it, and, in so doing, we mentally attach to it as well. It seems totally appropriate to hear our coaches screaming at us to "watch the ball!" or "concentrate on the ball!"

These familiar admonishments refer to attachment in its two most common forms: visual attachment and mental attachment. Think of it as the mind attaching to what the eyes are focused on, which is all fine-and-dandy until the object your eyes are focused on starts moving too fast to maintain an accurate visual attachment. That's when your eyes start giving your brain inaccurate visual information about the speed and direction of the object they are trying to follow, and that inaccurate visual input leads to inaccurate motor output, which, in turn, leads to negative contact, or worse, no contact at all. End result: you lose.

Every time you mishit a backhand in tennis, boot a ground ball in baseball, or miss a dig in volleyball, the root cause of your contact error can be traced back to an error in your visual input, an error that is directly related to your attachment to an object that is moving too fast for your eyes to follow using a serial input strategy. Fortunately we all have the ability to switch visual strategies, to detach from the action in our visual field by attaching our focus to the empty space of our contact zone. And while attaching to empty space is technically another form of attachment, what we are really attaching to is "nothing." No-thing. And attachment to nothing is non-attachment.

Attachment to "something" automatically places value on that "thing," and when we cannot have what we value, when we cannot have what we want, we experience suffering. The Great Wisdom Traditions all speak of detaching from the world of form and desire and looking instead to the world of emptiness wherein there is no attachment, no desire, and therefore no suffering.

The Wisdom Traditions might as well be talking about our visual and mental attachment to the objects of contact that we value so much in fast-moving contact sports. What do we want the most when we focus on the ball coming into our contact zone? Don't we want to control the ball and hit it right where we want it to go? Why do we focus on the ball if not to control the ball in one way or another? That desire to control the ball is causal to both our joy and suffering in ball sports, and that desire begins with our focal attachment to form.

In our daily lives as in our sports, we always want to take control of the action. Seen from the interior perspective of our wants and desires, our needs and values, focusing on the ball or our opponent or our target is all about wanting to feel a sense of control over our environment. The more control we have over our environment, the safer we feel, the more confident we feel, the more the self is satisfied. Conversely, the more we lose control of our environment, the less secure we feel, doubt enters in, and self suffers.

In his book *Big Mind – Big Heart, Finding Your Way,* Zen Master Dennis Genpo Merzel speaks directly to the issue of control by dialoguing directly with the voice of the "Controller:" (Merzel 71)

FACILITATOR: *May I speak to the Controller?*

CONTROLLER: *Yes, you're speaking to the Controller.*

FACILITATOR: *What's your function or job, how do you see yourself?*

CONTROLLER: *I'm here to control. I work very closely with the Protector. In fact my major job of controlling is in order to protect. Again, I basically have to protect him, the self, from others. Everything out there is potentially harmful and dangerous, and I have to be very vigilant, very attentive and aware. Of course I rely a lot on other voices, like Fear. But I have to control situations.*

FACILITATOR: *If you could, what would you control?*

CONTROLLER: *I'd control everything and everyone if I could. That would be ideal, if I could control everybody's actions, everybody's feelings, their thoughts, their emotions, how they express themselves, how they behave toward the self. If I could, I'd control the environment, the weather, how overcast, how much sunshine – obviously I'd like to control it all.*

Sound familiar?

Self plays a huge role in our performance, and how we deal with the different aspects of self, such as the "Controller," is vital to the quality of our performance. The Parallel Mode Process uses this need to control in a uniquely different way. Instead of trying to control the action in your athletic environment, you are invited to take control of your visual and mental focus as the action in your athletic environment arises in its moment-to-moment progression. In other words, give the Controller something to control – your focus.

Think of it this way: when you are focused on form, form is controlling your focus. When you are focused on the action in your athletic environment, the action is controlling your focus. Wouldn't you feel a greater sense of control if *you* were controlling your focus instead of letting your focus be controlled by the action in your environment? The Parallel Mode Process suggests that you take control of your own focus by putting it exactly where it will do you the most good – on your contact zone.

But there's a paradox involved: *you take control of your focus by defocusing.* You defocus from form and focus instead on empty space. That focal shift requires the Controller in you to stop trying to control what it *can't* control in the first place – the action in your athletic environment – and, instead, to start controlling something that it *can* control – your visual and mental focus. By fixing your focus on your contact zone you are keeping the Controller in you perpetually occupied doing a very important strategic task – the task of prefocusing on your contact zone. Remember, by prefocusing *on* your contact zone, you eliminate the need to refocus *to* your contact zone. *Prefocusing eliminates refocusing,* and when you eliminate the refocusing variable in fast-moving athletic environments, you eliminate the major cause of bad timing. (See The Contact Zone and Timing)

The Paradox of Control

It took more than a few months of me battling with my visual and mental focus before I was able to stay focused on my contact zone during competition, but from those battles there emerged a radically different sense of control, a sense of control that had little to do with controlling the action on the court and much to do with controlling my own focus amidst all the action taking place. Whenever I went back to focusing on the ball or my opponent or any of the action on the court, I immediately felt that sense of control slipping away into the chaos.

But when I got into flow, everything was reversed. *I was controlling my focus by defocusing!* But the more I thought about it, the more sense it made. By defocusing from the action in front of me, my focus was no longer being controlled by that action. Instead, I was taking control of my own focus and putting it on my contact zone. At first it felt like I was letting go of any and all control I had over the action, but the result was an ever-increasing sense of control over myself and what I was doing out there on the court. It all seemed backwards, like I was gaining control by giving up control. Paradox.

And here's the biggest paradox of all: by taking control of my own focus and fixing it on my contact zone, I was taking visual and mental control of the empty space of my contact zone, which, in reality, meant that I was taking control of "nothing." So instead of the Controller in me trying to take control of *everything* in order to perform at my highest level, I was experiencing my peak performance state when the Controller in me was taking control of *nothing*. More paradox.

And as I spent more and more time in the zone, I began to realize that there was something deeper going on, something that went beneath the greater sense of control I was feeling when I played, something that sat at the causal level and integrated all the interior and exterior characteristics of flow into a single transformative state, and it dealt directly with the spatiotemporal dimension of the present.

At its core, the Parallel Mode Process is about controlling your interior conscious state by controlling your exterior focal state, which is exactly what happens when you defocus from form and fix your focus on your contact zone. Focusing on empty space sits at the center of creating the unified spatiotemporal dimension of the present, and it is the present dimension that must be maintained in order to maintain flow. So the sense of control you feel when you're in a flow state has more to do with controlling flow's causal spatiotemporal dimension than with controlling the action in the environment. By maintaining a Parallel Mode of operation, you are not only maintaining simultaneous control over your exterior visual focus *and* your interior mental focus, you are also maintaining control over the present dimension, which is the only dimension in which flow occurs. In other words, when you maintain control of your Parallel Mode of operation, you are maintaining control of the flowing present.

That's huge! And it's the deeper reason you feel a greater sense of control when you are in the zone. You are actually controlling the spatiotemporal dimension that creates the zone. Why wouldn't you feel a greater sense of control? You're actually controlling the space and time of unified flowing presence! The control you have over the action in your environment is secondary. It seems to happen on its own without any effort from you. You *feel* in control without trying to *be* in control, and it all begins with control of the flowing present.

If there is a secret to playing in the zone at any skill level and in any sport, it's your ability to co-create and then maintain the spatiotemporal dimension of flowing presence while the action arises all around you in its moment-to-moment dance. When you are in the zone, you are in a one-to-one relationship with that dance, and there is no closer relationship that being one with your environment. That's when subject and object are no longer two, and where control is experienced in its transcendent form.

The act of controlling your focus by fixing it on your contact zone not only defocuses you from the material dimension of form and all the confusion that goes along with sequentially dissecting the action, but more importantly, focusing on empty space as form arises brings together all the sequential parts of the game into a simultaneous and unified whole; a unified reality that *transcends* the parts yet simultaneously *includes* the parts.

This is Presence. This is integral consciousness. This is flow.

Process and Outcome

Learning how to maintain a fixed-focus state was anything but easy for me. There were plenty of failures mixed in with the successes as I learned to control my focus. It took discipline and daily practice, but the payoff was always the same: a shift to a more comprehensive perspective in which I was able to see everything that was happening in front of me simultaneously. The biggest difference with this new visual perspective was just what you might imagine: maintaining a fixed-focus on my contact zone meant the people, objects, and targets in my visual field, although visible, were always out of focus, always a bit fuzzy.

To say that was strange is an understatement. Focusing on my contact zone was everything I was trained *not* to do as an athlete. But every time the ball moved closer to my contact zone, it also started moving *into* focus, so as it got closer, it also got clearer, and without any visual effort on my part. All I had to do was look along the surface of my imaginary window for the contact point and let the ball come into focus on its own.

But there was something of equal importance that always happened when I shifted into FDF and simply defended my imaginary window, and that was an immediate absence of concern for any outcome, positive or negative. As long as I played this imaginary game, I was no longer attached to the outcome of my shots. Instead, I felt an immediate sense of freedom, as if I was loosed from some invisible cage that had kept me locked inside my own performance inhibitions and insecurities.

Conventional wisdom has always maintained that in order to perform to your full potential in any endeavor, you have to *stay in the process and stay out of the outcome*, and that's exactly what I found myself doing. Whenever I played this game of defending my imaginary window with my racquet, there was no outcome, only the process of defending my window with my racquet. End of story. End of process. If I was successful, I said yes; if the ball got past my window, I said no. That's it. That's all I did. And when that was all I did, I always felt unencumbered, uninhibited, suddenly freed from the burden of outcome.

I was still *peripherally aware* of the outcome, mind you. I could still see everything that was happening after I contacted the ball, I just wasn't focused on it. Instead, I was leaving my focus on my contact zone as the ball moved away and into the simultaneous mix of action that was continuously arising in my visual field. Furthermore, when I stayed focused on my contact zone, I was always ready for the next ball that came my way, and in tennis, like many other sports, the next action can come your way in a very big hurry. Staying in the process and out of the outcome makes dealing with the next action a lot easier, and staying focused on your contact zone makes staying in the process a very real experience.

Duality vs. Unity in Sport

What I have come to realize over the years of teaching athletes how to get in the zone is that everyone is capable of playing their chosen sport in a state of flow; everyone is capable of creating a unified reality in their athletic environment, but because we are so conditioned to dualistic thinking, subject-object thinking, we find it difficult to shift out of this dualistic mindset. It's not that we can't, it's just that we are uncomfortable letting go of our dualistic interface.

This problem is directly related to the way we use our eyes as we flit from one fixation point to another, visually jumping from object to object in our visual field. Dualistic thinking is interior, and with that interior dualism there is a corresponding exterior dualism created by sequentially focusing our eyes from object to object, a serial input pattern that literally separates our environment into sequential bits and pieces while separating us from each of those pieces.

Contrast the dualism of serial input with the unification of parallel input wherein you focus on the empty space of your contact zone, and, in so doing, defocus from the objects in your visual field. But remember, defocusing from the objects in your visual field *does not make them invisible,* just out of focus. You don't lose sight of anything. In fact, while you are focused on nothing, you still see everything!

No matter what your sport, shifting to this parallel or unified interface will feel very strange at first, but with practice, connecting to the unified whole of your environment will give you a very real sense of oneness with your game. This sense of oneness is a characteristic of flowing presence, and it's the flowing presence you co-create by interfacing with the past and the future equally and simultaneously. Flowing presence and unified reality are one and the same.

The Parallel Mode Process suggests that you access the flowing presence of your sport by directly connecting to it with your sensorimotor operating system. That's the beauty of the human operating system. It is capable of creating either a serial interface with its environment or a parallel interface with the same environment. But when you create a parallel interface with the environment, you not only change yourself, you also change the environment; it's no longer the same as it was.

With a serial interface you experience the parts of the environment individually and sequentially, while with a parallel interface you experience the whole of the environment equally and simultaneously with all the individual parts included in the whole. Two radically different operational interfaces, with each creating a different exterior reality as well as a different interior awareness. One operational interface creates an exterior reality in which the parts are primary to the whole. The other operational interface creates an exterior reality in which the whole is primary to, but includes, the parts. One reality is dualistic, the other unified. In one reality subject and object are two. In the other, subject and object are not two.

As I was developing this process, what I found happening along the way was that the process itself was also developing me in ways I never knew were there. Mostly, this process taught me that I had a choice in the reality I was creating in my sport of tennis. I could choose to create a dualistic reality by connecting to the game in a Serial Mode – which was my old way of playing the game – or I could choose to create a unified reality by connecting to the game in a Parallel Mode – which was not only becoming my new way of playing the game, but was also developing into a new way of teaching the game, and the more I learned how to teach the Parallel Mode Process, the more I realized that we all have the ability to connect with the unified reality of our various sports, but because we are so conditioned to living our daily lives in a dualistic/serial interface, we end up playing our sports in the same way. We experience a dualistic athletic environment because we actively connect to it in a dualistic/serial interface. And for many, this dualistic experience seems like the only true reality there is.

It is not. We are also capable of creating a different reality, a unified reality that involves a one-to-one interface with the full-potential of our sport. The evidence that we are able to create and then function in this one-to-one interface is exhibited every time we get in the zone as athletes. Shifting to a Parallel Mode is a way to immediately access this unified experience in our various sports, and the reason it works for all sports, all skill levels, all ages, and across all cultural boundaries and stages of athletic development is because we are all, first and foremost, human beings, which means we all operate in essentially the same way.

We are all systems of countermovement interfacing with and within a larger system of movement (R-fields), and as human beings, we can choose to create a dualistic reality through the use of a serial interface, or we can choose to create a unified reality through the use of a parallel interface. Each interface gives us a different athletic experience, and the fact that we can choose which interface we use when we compete means that we can choose to compete in our normal performance state or we can choose to compete in our peak performance state. *We can literally choose to compete in a state of flow.* The challenge lies in shifting from the habituated duality of a serial interface to the unified reality of a parallel interface.

The Call of the Zone

The conscious state that creates the most complete picture of your athletic reality is the conscious state that includes an equal and simultaneous combination of form and empty space – past and future – in a *nondominant* interface; an interface in which neither form nor empty space dominates your reality, but rather both are integrated into a unified whole that is the complete reality in which and with which you experience your peak performance state, and with that experience comes not only an awakening to the full-potential of the athletic environment, but also an awakening to your Authentic Self.

The two go together; you can't have one without the other. If it were possible to get in the zone in your gross conscious state, then human peak performance would certainly be a lot easier and a lot less mysterious. But that's not the way it happens. The exterior correlate of your gross conscious state is a Serial Mode of operation, and because a Serial Mode of operation is neither as efficient nor as accurate as a Parallel Mode of operation, you can never play to your full potential in your gross conscious state.

Never.

Don't get me wrong. You can perform at a very high level in a gross conscious state with its corresponding Serial Mode of operation, but gross consciousness is neither as comprehensive nor as all-inclusive as integral consciousness, so no matter how well you perform in a gross conscious state with its Serial Mode of operation, it will never reach the level of performance you can achieve in a state of integral consciousness with its corresponding Parallel Mode of operation.

Making the shift from gross to integral consciousness requires a shift from serial to parallel operation, and that exterior shift in operation begins with a shift in your focal connection to the R-field environment. You have to let go of your variable-focus connection to the differentiated parts of your R-field environment in favor of a fixed-focus connection to the undifferentiated whole. That's the long way of saying that in order to shift into your Parallel Mode of operation you have to slam the door shut on your Serial Mode, and the best reason to leave your Serial Mode behind is that a unified connection to the whole functions more effectively than a dualistic connection to the parts.

So, when it comes to performance, there are some very logical reasons for making the shift from your Serial Mode to your Parallel Mode. But the fundamental reason for making the shift lies in a single, undeniable truth: *playing in the present is more effective than playing in the past,* and when you shift into your Parallel Mode, you stop playing in the past and start playing in the present, and that, just that, is the clarion call of the zone.

The Search

Flow motivates us as athletes. We know the zone exists. We know it because we've glimpsed it on those rare occasions when everything comes together, and for a brief moment of performance harmony, we glimpse the unified reality of our sport. Then it goes away as mysteriously as it came, leaving us wondering what happened and how can we make it happen again? Thus begins our search for the mysterious and elusive zone.

When we consult the experts in the field, they tell us we can't make flow happen by choice, we can only prepare for it. Flow happens only by chance, as if it has a mind of its own and we have nothing to say in the matter. So we continue the search and we end up searching in all the wrong places, not knowing that what we seek was never really lost. What we seek is always there. Always was, always is, and always will be. And it is always there because it is timeless. What we seek is ever-present because it is exactly that – the present dimension – the spatiotemporal dimension that is always already here – right here, right now. In other words, what we seek – the present dimension – was never lost in the first place. *THE FLOWING PRESENT*

What *is* lost, however, is our *connection* to flowing presence, and when we find this connection, whether consciously or unconsciously, we also find the zone. And as long as we maintain our direct connection to flowing presence, we also maintain our highest level of performance. But the instant we break that connection, we immediately lose our flow state, we immediately come out of the zone and return to the ups and downs of our normal performance reality. *YES!*

And the search is on again – the search for that which was never lost in the first place. It's still right where it was, right where it is, right where

STAYING IN THE NOW

it always will be. It's still right here, right now in the present moment, and it cannot be found by searching for it.

It can, however, be found by connecting to it.

When you are in flow, you are directly connected to and interfacing with and within the spatiotemporal dimension of the present. You don't find it, you connect to what is always here, and through that connection you co-create the unified realty of the present dimension.

That, just that, is flow.

Here's the truth about flow: *it cannot be lost because the present dimension cannot be lost.* We can, and do, lose our connection to the present moment, and when we disconnect from the present, we also disconnect from flow's ultimate performance reality. This happens to all of us, no matter what our level of skill or stage of athletic development. Thus, the zone continues to elude and baffle us as athletes. We refer to it as "playing unconsciously" or "playing out of our minds." The fact that we experience the zone on rare occasions, the fact that we *do* have brief glimpses of flow, makes us feel like it is something we can find again if we just keep searching…and searching…and searching. But searching is the problem not the solution, especially when our search is centered in the material world of form. It's like searching for the missing piece of the performance puzzle – the perfect technique, the perfect equipment, the perfect coach, or the perfect system – something we can find "out there" that will make us whole "in here."

See the problem?

Here's a different perspective. You are already whole "in here." You already have the perfect technique, you already own the perfect equipment, you already have the perfect coach, and you already possess the perfect system.

The perfect system is your own operating system, and it is already whole. It is already capable of directly connecting to the whole of its athletic environment. It is already capable of the perfect technique for creating a unified connection to the reality of flowing presence. You already have the perfect equipment for making that unified connection – your sensorimotor operating system. And you are already capable of interfacing with and within the whole of your athletic reality. Most importantly, you already have the perfect coach – your Authentic Self.

So everything you are searching for out there is already in here, right here, right now, in this and every present moment. It's your Authentic Self in the here and now. The Authentic Self you've been searching for in all the wrong places. The Authentic Self that cannot be found because it has never been lost. The Authentic Self, like flowing presence, is always already here. The Authentic Self is the *whole* you coming out to play whenever you connect to the *whole* of your athletic environment. Any separation from the whole comes from playing your games in a Serial Mode. Yet after years of asymmetrically focusing only on form, we naturally take our dualistic conditioning into the games we play, connecting only partially to the whole of our athletic environment, and with that partial connection comes the sense that something is missing. We feel incomplete, unfulfilled, always wondering what's missing from our game. And we search for what's missing by further dissecting our game into its component parts. Maybe if we chop our game into smaller and smaller pieces we'll finally come across the missing piece. It's got to be hidden away in there somewhere, right?

But flow is not hidden at all. It's ever-present. Right here, right now, always and already with us and within us. We just have to connect directly to its ever-present, unified reality through the use parallel interface. Make the direct connection and you awaken not only your peak performance state, you also awaken your Authentic Self. It's just that easy.

But it's oh, so very, very hard. OR NOT

The Contact Zone and Timing

Playing in the zone is not just about higher consciousness and sport. It's also about peak performance. It's about playing your sport at a higher level – immediately. And one of the main reasons you experience an immediate improvement in your performance is that when you shift into your Parallel Mode of operation, your *timing* improves immediately.

My initial reason for visualizing a big imaginary window in front of me was not because I knew it would shift me into the zone. I had no idea that would happen. My initial reason was that my timing was off, and I figured that if I contacted the ball *at* my imaginary window, then my timing would be good, but if I contacted the ball *behind* my imaginary window, then my timing would be bad.

Contact at my window   →   good timing.
Contact behind my window   →   bad timing.

That simple definition of timing not only gave me a way to quickly explain timing to my students, but it also gave me a way to introduce them to their peak performance state without any mention of playing "in the zone." Remember, back in the late 70's any talk of playing in the zone was still considered taboo, so instead of linking visualization and imaginary windows with playing in the zone, I began using the imaginary window idea as a "timing tool," a way to objectively measure the location of contact relative to a *predefined depth of contact*.

Once players began seeing the positive results that came with making consistent contact at a predefined depth of contact, getting them to focus on their contact zone became a means to an end, a logical process by which they could improve their timing and thereby improve their performance. But here's the best part: as their timing improved, so did their performance, and as their performance improved, so did their willingness to defocus from form and focus instead on the empty space of their contact zone. And as they shifted into FDF and their Parallel Mode of operation, they also shifted into the zone. It was like introducing athletes to the zone by taking them through a back door entrance that was completely logical and dealt directly with improving their performance. It was the back door of timing.

I found, however, that using a large window as a visual representation of the contact zone wasn't enough to explain the variables of timing. Timing needed a more expansive definition, so I went about expanding my simple definition of timing by expanding my definition of the contact zone itself.

Here's an expanded look at the contact zone as I explain it in tennis, but this explanation can be applied to all sports involving movement, countermovement, and contact:

Snapshot of the Contact Zone

Imagine one window spanning the court in front of you at a comfortable arm's distance and another imaginary window of the same dimensions located right against your body. Now you have two windows

– a front window representing the front side of your contact zone, a middle area of your contact zone, and a back window representing the back side of your contact zone. This extra window gives you a 3-dimensional contact zone containing height, width, and depth, and by assigning numbers to the different depths of the contact zone, you can measure the relative timing of your contact according to the location of your contact points.

Here's the numbering system I started using and still use to this day. The front side of the contact zone is a 3-Depth. The middle of the contact zone is a 2-Depth. The back side of the contact zone is a 1-Depth. 3 – 2 – 1. Easy to understand in any language, and an easy way to measure your own timing in whatever sport you play.

Positive, Neutral, and Negative Timing

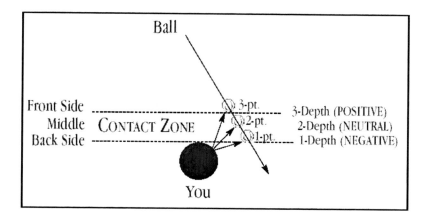

Every object of movement that enters your contact zone can be contacted by your countermovement at a contact point located at one of these three contact depths. You can make contact at the front side of your contact zone – a 3-Depth/3-Point. You can also make contact in the middle of your contact zone – at a 2-Depth/2-Point. Or, you could make contact at the back side of your contact zone –at a 1-Depth/1-Point.

The location of each contact point gives you a way to objectively measure the relationship of your countermovements to the movement of the ball, or any object as it moves through your contact zone, and from those measurements you can deduce certain basic facts about your timing. For instance: contact at a 3-Depth/3-Point means that your countermovement was in full control of the contact zone; movement never penetrated the contact zone. Contact occurred at the exact point in space and time that the ball first arrived at the contact zone, the *Primary Contact Point*, or, in this measuring system, the 3-Point. Contact at the 3-Point is *Positive Timing*.

If contact occurs at a 2-Depth/2-Point, then movement penetrated and controlled the front half of the contact zone, the positive or offensive half, while your countermovement controlled the back half of the contact zone, the negative or defensive half. Contact at the 2-Point is *Neutral Timing.*

Contact at a 1-Depth/1-Point means that movement was in complete control of the contact zone while your countermovement never entered into the contact zone at all. Contact at the 1-Point is *Negative Timing.*

- Contact at the 3-Point = Positive Timing
- Contact at the 2-Point = Neutral Timing
- Contact at the 1-Point = Negative Timing

Positive Contact

More often than not, with Positive Timing you get *Positive Contact*. Positive Contact is contact that produces a positive outcome – a base hit in baseball, a solid tackle in football, a dead-solid perfect 3-iron in golf – all products of Positive Contact.

Conversely, *Negative Contact* is contact that produces a negative outcome – a muffed ground ball in softball, an unforced error in tennis, or a duck-hook in golf – all products of Negative Contact.

The third contact option is *No Contact*. In any contact sequence sport, No Contact is a losing proposition. Think of striking out and you get the picture of No Contact.

So Positive Contact creates a positive outcome while Negative Contact and No Contact both create negative outcomes. As obvious as that sounds, what is not so obvious is the fact that all three of these *contact potentials* always exist in the space and time of your contact zone. Located somewhere in that empty space is the Primary Contact Point, the point of Positive Timing, the 3-Point in our measuring system, the point at which Positive Contact is most often created, and by focusing on your contact zone, by using FDF as your visual input pattern, your chances of locating the 3-Point are much greater than if you are focused on the object of contact itself, especially if that object is moving at a high rate of speed.   *AMEN!*

FDF not only increases the likelihood of making contact at the 3-Point, which, in turn, increases the likelihood of creating Positive Contact, but FDF is also the visual input pattern of the zone, and it can be used in any sport, at any skill level, and at any stage of athletic development. You don't have to be an elite athlete to get in the zone. You don't have to master the techniques of your sport before you can experience flow. You don't have to be accomplished at what you do; you just have to be willing to change the way you do it. You have to be willing to change the way you visually connect to your athletic environment, and that visual change does not come easily for most athletes. In fact, it might be the hardest thing you ever do.

The payoff, however, is big time. The payoff is flow, and whether you're a beginner, a recreational player, or a professional athlete, playing your sport in a flow state is as good as it gets. The question is: are you willing to pay the price? Are you willing to change the way you visually connect to the game? Are you willing to defocus from the action and focus instead on your contact zone? Are you willing to defocus from form and focus instead on empty space?

If you are, then a unified performance reality awaits you, right here, right now. All you have to do is connect to it. But if you're unwilling to change the way you connect to the game, then that unified performance reality is still right here, still right now, only you won't be aware of it because you won't be connected to it. You won't experience the unified whole because you are too busy connecting to the sequential parts.

But the whole is always there, always was, always is, always will be. You can't get rid of the whole; you can only separate from it by connecting sequentially to the parts. The Parallel Mode Process suggests that you stop connecting to the parts and start connecting to the whole as the parts arise in your moment-to-moment awareness.

How do you connect to the whole? How do you connect to everything at the same time? Simple – by connecting to nothing. By focusing on the empty space of your contact zone as the action arises sequentially right before your eyes.

Immediacy

Up to this point, most of the emphasis has been on the upper quadrants of Wilber's AQAL framework: the interior conscious state of the individual athlete – Upper Left quadrant – and the individual athlete's exterior mode of operation – Upper Right quadrant.

Quick Review: the athlete in a gross state of consciousness (interior) and a Serial Mode of operation (exterior) is playing in his/her normal performance state while the athlete in a state of integral consciousness (interior) and Parallel Mode of operation (exterior) is playing in his/her peak performance state.

Gross Interior / Serial Mode Exterior = Normal Performance State
Integral Interior / Parallel Mode Exterior = Peak Performance State

Structurally, these are the individual interior and exterior differences between playing in the norm and playing in the zone, and they are major differences, core structural changes that require dedicated practice and perseverance to stabilize and develop. You won't master flow overnight. In fact, you might never master flow, but mastery is not the objective of the practice. The practice itself is the objective. To practice the Parallel Mode Process is to practice flowing presence in your sport, and with that practice you will get better at co-creating and stabilizing the present dimension as you play. And best of all, the more you practice playing your sport in the zone; the more familiar you will become with your Authentic Self.

You've probably heard the phrase: "it's about the journey not the destination," but when your practice involves shifting into the zone, you get the journey *and* the destination at the same time! The Parallel Mode

Process is the journey, and with that journey comes unified performance reality – the destination. The zone is not some future destination that you might someday find if you diligently continue your practice. On the contrary, the experience of the zone is right here, right now, in the present dimension, and as a destination, that's the only way the zone can be experienced – right here, right now. The journey itself is a journey of flowing presence, and it happens immediately when you shift into a Parallel Mode of operation.

When I first started teaching tennis players how to get in the zone, I found this immediacy to be a powerful attraction. Within minutes, players of all levels were getting in the zone. Then it was just a matter of letting the experience speak for itself. I didn't have to say much of anything once a player shifted into the zone. In fact, the less I said the better. My teaching rapidly moved away from teaching players the techniques of how to play tennis into teaching players the techniques of how to co-create and stabilize the zone while they played tennis.

Again, it wasn't about the tennis as much as it was about shifting into the zone while playing tennis. Tennis was included, but the whole experience transcended tennis. Tennis became a vehicle for awakening players to their own true nature. Of course, it didn't hurt that along the way this immediate experience of awakening to one's own true nature also included an immediate experience of playing one's socks off! None of this would have worked if players didn't play better, and play better immediately. Why would anyone try something as radically different as the Parallel Mode Process if it didn't work better than what they were doing – and work better immediately?

But that is the only way the experience of flowing presence can work. It has to work *immediately.* It has to work right here, right now. Anything else is bogus, a fraud, a lie. And there is nothing but truth to be found in flowing presence – the truth of who you really are. The strength of the Parallel Mode Process lies in this immediacy. You don't have to be a skilled athlete

RADIX = ROOT

or a skilled meditator to have an immediate experience of flow, and it was the immediacy of this flow experience that radically changed my approach to teaching tennis. Why make players wait around for years to experience the zone when they could create that experience immediately?

Nowadays, I find that a growing number of people – athletes and non-athletes alike – are looking for something more from life, a practice that will enable them to experience the freedom and fullness that life has to offer. Sport can provide such a practice. Sport can be the vehicle for exploring life's higher-order realities, and the Parallel Mode Process gives people a way to explore those realities sooner rather than later. I've witnessed total beginners to tennis experiencing the game's unified reality right from the get-go, and watched as they came face-to-face with their own true nature.

And it happens immediately. In fact, when athletes from another sport – say baseball – ask to see what this zone stuff is all about, I don't try to explain how to play baseball in the zone. Instead I get them on the tennis court and within minutes they are playing tennis in the zone. Within minutes they are having a first-hand experience of flow, and once they feel what it's like to hit a tennis ball in the zone, it's pretty easy to translate that feeling into hitting a baseball in the zone.

Over the years, I've used tennis to introduce flow to athletes in many different sports ranging from football to baseball, to soccer, volleyball, lacrosse, golf, cycling, running, basketball, archery, martial arts, and bowling – yes, bowling – just about every sport there is, and I always introduce the athletes to the flow experience first through tennis, then we translate to their particular sport.

Here's the reason: tennis has a very special trait that makes it a perfect vehicle for introducing athletes to flow, and that trait is the rapid repetition of contact sequences. One contact sequence follows another, then another, generally in three seconds or less, which means you have very little time to think between contact sequences, very little time to analyze, very little time to judge; you only have time enough to do, only time enough to use your tennis racquet to keep the oncoming ball from breaking through your imaginary window. Only time enough to say "yes" is you are successful or "no," if you are not.

With tennis there is only enough time for action and immediate feedback. And that immediate verbal feedback comes every three seconds or less – again, and again, and again – as the ball is hit back and forth across the net in a highly controlled situation we call "mini tennis" or "dink tennis."

Anyone can grab a tennis racquet and put it flat up against a wall. All you need after that is a follow-through. The "forehand stroke" in tennis is similar to grabbing a tennis racquet and putting it against a flat surface like a wall – or an imaginary window – and then following through. This simple countermovement is all it takes to hit a tennis ball over the net in mini tennis. Something anyone can do. Defensive linemen can do it, wide receivers can do it, pitchers and catchers can do it, gymnasts can do it, lacrosse and hockey goalies can do it, techies can do it, academics with no athletic background can do it – the point being, the basic forehand stroke in tennis is something anyone can do because anyone can grab a flat object like a tennis racquet, put it flat against a wall, and then follow-through. Take that basic technique onto the tennis court and you've got a simple forehand stroke that can keep oncoming tennis balls from getting past your imaginary window.

- First comes the movement of the ball toward your imaginary window.
- Then comes your countermovement to prevent the ball from getting past your imaginary window by putting your racquet flat against your window at the contact point.
- Then comes contact at the window with *vertically aligned racquet strings.*
- Then comes the follow-through.

Guess what happens when you contact a tennis ball with vertically aligned racquet strings? The tennis ball goes back over the net. And it continues to go back over the net – again, and again, and again.

"Yes." "Yes." "Yes." Immediate verbal feedback. Again, and again, and again.

Very soon your eyes settle into focusing on the imaginary window you are visualizing and defending with your racquet. Very soon your eyes relax into a FDF input pattern and your operating system shifts into its Parallel Mode of operation, and all you are doing is keeping one ball after another from getting past your imaginary window. And with that exterior shift into a Parallel Mode of operation comes an interior shift into a state of integral consciousness.

Within minutes you are "in the zone."

Over the years, I've taught a wide spectrum of athletes how to get in the zone by starting them off with mini-tennis using simple forehand and backhand techniques and putting them into action in a controlled environment of moderated speeds and distances. And I've seen them all shift into FDF and a Parallel Mode of operation within minutes. And with the shift in their exterior mode from serial to parallel operation comes the simultaneous shift in their interior state from gross to integral consciousness.

Presto! Just like that – they're in the zone. And it never fails!

Athletes and academics alike; it never fails. The immediacy of the contact sequence experience coupled with the immediacy of the "yes/no" verbal feedback – again and again and again – every three seconds or less, keeps players totally focused on the objective of defending their imaginary window with simple forehand and backhand techniques.

It also keeps them playing mini-tennis "in the zone."

Baby steps – we start with baby steps. Playing mini-tennis in the zone is something anyone can do, and by including immediate verbal feedback on the maintenance of the task at hand, you are giving yourself immediate, first-person verification of the fact that you are co-creating and maintaining the peak performance experience of flow. It's not uncommon to see a rank beginner with no athletic background hit 20 to 30 balls back and forth over the net in less than half an hour. That means they are maintaining flow for the length of time it takes to hit 20 to 30 balls in a row back and forth across the net. That's approximately one minute of playing mini-tennis in the zone.

- That's one minute of one human being co-creating a unified performance reality.
- That's one minute of experiencing one's own true nature.
- That's one minute of awakening to one's Authentic Self.

One minute doesn't sound like much, does it? One minute of *anything* doesn't sound like much. But this isn't one minute of anything. This is one minute of *everything*. One minute of everything the environment has to offer you, and one minute of everything you have to offer the environment. That translates to one minute of a one-to-one connection with the whole.

That very connection, just that, can change the way you see yourself, and it can change the way you see the world. Or, you can keep thinking that it's just something strange that happens for no apparent reason.

Attentional Theory and the Zone

The Random House Dictionary defines attention as: "the act or faculty of mentally concentrating on a single object, thought, or event, especially in preference to other stimuli". (http://dictionary.reference.com/browse/attention.)

Ask any athlete in any fast-moving ball sport to name the single most important object on which they mentally concentrate and the answer is always the same: *the ball.* We are taught from day-one to concentrate on the ball, to focus our attention on the ball, to watch the ball, even to "be the ball," which is great advice if we are being taught how to play that sport "in the norm."

Watching the ball, focusing on the ball, mentally attending to the ball, or even being the ball is a sure-fire way to lock ourselves into a VDF input pattern and a Serial Mode of operation. And, remember, if our Upper Right quadrant, exterior mode of operation is a Serial Mode, then its Upper Left quadrant, interior correlate is going to be a *gross conscious state,* our normal conscious state. Together the Upper-Left and Upper-Right quadrants combine to co-create the structure of our individual performance state, and if that structure is a combination of Gross Interior and Serial Mode Exterior, then we are literally locking ourselves into our normal performance state:

Gross Interior / Serial Mode Exterior = Normal Performance State

If we want to play our sport in our peak performance state, then we have to shift into the structure of peak performance:

Integral Interior / Parallel Mode Exterior = Peak Performance State

And that means shifting the way we focus our eyes *and* shifting the way we focus our minds. In other words, we have to make a shift in the focus of our attention.

Attentional Theory suggests that if we want to play our sport "in the zone," then that shift in our focus should take place along the continuum of a *Broad External* focus of attention to a *Narrow External* focus of attention.

Here's what that means:

Attentional theory states that an athlete's attention can be at any place on two separate continuums of attention. One continuum involves an *External* or *Internal* focus of attention, while the second continuum involves a *Broad* or *Narrow* focus of attention. When these two continuums are crossed, four quadrants of attention are created (more quadrants!).

Each attentional quadrant deals with the type of task athletes perform while their attention is in that quadrant. Here's a graphic illustration of that concept:

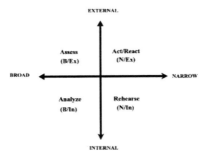

Matthew Krug, in his 1999 internet article "*Playing Tennis In The Zone*" clearly defined the differences between the four attentional quadrants using a female athlete in his example:

The broad external quadrant (B/Ex) is being used when (1) the athlete's attention lies outside of her body and (2) she is examining a large number of cues. This quadrant allows her to assess the environment, searching for task relevant cues. The narrow external quadrant (N/Ex) is being used when (1) the athlete's attention lies outside of her body and (2) she is examining a limited number of cues. This quadrant allows her to act and react to the environmental cues.

The broad internal quadrant (B/In) is being used when (1) the athlete's attention lies inside her body and (2) she is examining a large number of cues. When the athlete is analyzing strategy for the upcoming game, she will be using the broad internal quadrant. The narrow internal quadrant (N/In) is being used when (1) the athlete's attention lies inside her body and (2) the athlete is examining a limited number of cues. The athlete uses this quadrant when she visualizes or images her performance.

(Krug, http://www.athleticinsight.com/Vol1Iss3/Tennis_Zone.htm)

To summarize:

- Broad External (B/Ex): attention outside body, examining a large number of cues.
- Narrow External (N/Ex): attention outside body, examining a limited number of cues.
- Broad Internal (B/In): attention inside body, examining a large number of cues.
- Narrow Internal (N/In): attention inside body, examining a limited number of cues.

Attentional theory suggests that in order to maintain the zone, athletes in any sport must immerse themselves as much as possible in an *external focus of attention* and shift along that external continuum *between a broad and narrow focus.*

Krug then gives an example demonstrating how tennis players use all four attentional quadrants during the course of a point, but if you look closely, you will notice that when the ball is served in her direction, the tennis player in this example is playing tennis in a Serial Mode of operation. In other words, she is playing tennis *in the norm* NOT *in the zone.*

A tennis player is in the match, ready to return her opponent's serve. First she analyzes where her opponent may serve the ball. To perform this task, she must assess her opponent's tendencies and previous serves (broad internal). She then visualizes her return before stepping to the baseline (narrow internal). Once on the line, she analyzes the task relevant cues, her opponent, and the environmental conditions (broad external). **Her opponent serves the ball, and she focuses on the ball approaching her own racquet (narrow external).** *[emphasis added]*

Notice what she is doing with her focus when the ball is coming in her direction. She is *focusing on the ball.* She is *watching the ball.* She is visually and mentally focusing her attention on the object of movement and, in so doing, she is using a VDF visual input pattern, a serial input pattern in which her focus of attention is locked in the *narrow external* quadrant.

This is the way tennis players typically shift between the attentional quadrants when they are playing a match in their normal performance state. This is how athletes in all fast-moving ball sports are taught to shift their focus, and while there is nothing wrong with shifting back and forth between attentional quadrants, attentional theory itself suggests that too much time spent in the internal continuum is counterproductive to high level performance.

Internal focus, either broad or narrow, is fine as long as it's done between points. Internal thoughts, however, can lead to over-analysis, fear of failure, performance anxiety, and suddenly the attentional pattern necessary for peak performance is nowhere to be found. The question is: what attentional pattern is necessary for peak performance? What does attentional theory suggest we use as our pattern of focus if we want to play our chosen sport in the zone?

In a sport like tennis, attentional theory suggests that being in the zone involves the maintenance of an attentional pattern in which our focus of attention flows back and forth between a broad external focus of attention and a narrow external focus of attention as the ball moves back and forth across the net. In other words, to be in the zone in tennis, our focus of attention should looks like this:

Broad External → Narrow External → Broad External → Narrow External

Fixed-Depth of Focus and Attentional Theory

When I first show athletes how to shift into the zone, the emphasis is always on the different way in which they are using their eyes, more specifically, the shift from their normal visual input pattern of VDF to the radically different visual input pattern of FDF.

This reason there is so much emphasis on FDF is that the FDF visual input pattern mirrors the focusing pattern required to maintain the zone as defined by attentional theory. FDF is a focusing pattern in which the focus of your attention flows back and forth between a broad external focus of attention (focus on your window/contact zone) and a narrow external focus of attention (locate the contact point on your window).

When you visualize an imaginary window in front of you, you are focusing both your visual and mental attention on your contact zone, which automatically shifts you into a broad external focus of attention, a focus of attention in which *your attention lies outside your body and you are examining a large number of cues.*

Then, as you look for the contact point along the surface of your imaginary window, your attention flows smoothly from a broad external focus (contact zone) to a narrow external focus (contact point) in which *your attention lies outside your body, but you are examining a limited number of cues.*

Then, after contacting the ball at your window, instead of focusing on the ball as it goes back over the net (which would keep you in a narrow external focus of attention), you maintain a fixed focus on your contact zone and your attention flows smoothly back from narrow external focus to broad external focus.

With FDF, the pattern of focus looks like this:

Contact Zone → Contact Point → Contact Zone → Contact Point

Which mirrors this pattern of attention:

Broad External → Narrow External → Broad External → Narrow External

This pattern of attention flows smoothly across the external continuum from broad to narrow, broad to narrow, continuously repeating itself as you maintain a fixed-focus on the empty space of your contact zone and continue to locate each successive contact point upon its arrival at your imaginary window.

With FDF, you remain immersed in an external focus as your focus shifts along the external continuum between a broad and narrow focus of attention.

FDF is not only the visual input pattern that *shifts you into the zone*, but, according to attentional theory, FDF is also the visual input pattern that *keeps you immersed in the zone.*

Broad External → Narrow External → Broad External → Narrow External
Contact Zone → Contact Point → Contact Zone → Contact Point

This attentional pattern, no more, no less, is not only the attentional pattern for playing tennis in the zone; it is also the attentional pattern for playing any contact sequence sport in the zone.

Attention and Awareness

In contact sequence sports like tennis or baseball or volleyball or soccer, awareness means not only being aware of your own location on the court or on the field, but also being aware of the rest of the action taking place in front of you, in particular, the primary action of the ball's movement. With FDF, not only are you aware of the primary action arising in front of you – the movement of the ball – but you are also aware of the secondary action as it continues to arise in its moment-to-moment dance. FDF allows you to broadly examine all of the cues in your visual field simultaneously, and then narrow it down to the most essential cue of all – the location of the Primary Contact Point.

With VDF, on the other hand, you are continuously and sequentially refocusing on the various parts of the action on the court, which keeps you locked in a narrow external focus of attention, limiting your court or field awareness by limiting the number of cues you are examining. In fact, every time you shift your focus from one object to another (ball to opponent to target, etc.), you are sequentially shifting your focus from one narrow external cue to another, failing to open your focus to the larger number of cues simultaneously available to you should you shift to a broad external focus of attention.

Your field awareness, your court awareness, or any other form of situational awareness is severely limited when you remain in a narrow external focus of attention and continuously shift your focus from one piece of the action to another. It's like sequential tunnel vision. Watch your opponent! Watch the ball! Focus on your target! Focus on your shot! Attend to this! Attend to that! Suddenly, you're faced with too much information and not enough processing time. End result: you momentarily lose track of the primary object of movement, and that moment's loss of attention in fast-moving contact sports is all it takes to mess up the timing of your countermovements, i.e. negative timing. And negative timing is often accompanied by negative contact, or worse yet, no contact at all.

Unfortunately, VDF input with its narrow external focus of attention is the norm in sports training and sports coaching. It's the way we are taught to focus by well-meaning coaches who were taught to focus the same way by their well-meaning coaches who were also taught to focus the same way...well, you get the picture. It's like generational ignorance of the facts. One coaching generation after another passing down the same misinformation they received about how to use your eyes in fast-moving, contact sequence sports: focus on the ball, focus on form. That's it. That's how you do it. I know it's true because my coach told me so, and his coach told him the same thing, so it's got to be true.

Not so! The oldest misconception in ball sports is that focusing on the ball is the only way to use your eyes. Even though focusing on the ball *sounds* completely rational, focusing on the object of contact in any contact sport is a VDF visual input pattern, and any input pattern in which you are forced to constantly refocus your eyes in an effort to keep an object in focus as it moves around in your visual field also *keeps you immersed in a narrow external focus of attention*, whose very nature limits the number of cues you can examine in your visual field, which, in turn, limits your situational awareness. So while paying attention to the object of contact might sound like the most rational way to use your focus, it is actually the most limiting.

When athletes make the shift from VDF to FDF, the visual inaccuracies inherent to VDF's narrow external pattern of serial input are replaced with FDF's highly accurate broad to narrow external pattern of locating the Primary Contact Point along a predefined depth of contact– their imaginary window. This increased accuracy in the visual input pattern results in an immediately noticeable increase in the accuracy of the athlete's motor output that results in a countermovement that is positively timed. And, as we all know, a well-timed countermovement in any contact sport usually produces solid contact: a solid tackle in football, a solid hit in baseball, a solid kick in soccer, a solid spike in volleyball, and yes, even golf's ever-elusive, dead-solid perfect 3-iron is possible when you include a little positive timing!

Getting into the zone in your chosen sport requires not just a high level of concentration and focus; it requires a specific pattern of concentration and focus that shifts smoothly along the conscious continuum from a broad-external to a narrow-external focus of attention. How to actively implement this very specific attentional pattern has never before been defined as precisely as it is defined in the Parallel Mode Process performance model. Learning to use FDF as your visual input pattern is learning to use an input pattern that directly mirrors the focusing pattern of human peak performance as suggested by modern attentional theory.

As is always the case, however, how you use your eyes is up to you.

Linear and Non-Linear System Dynamics

Coaching in the West in the late 70's and early 80's was centered on the science of "biomechanics." Sport biomechanics is a combination of kinesiology, anatomy, physics, and technology, and has done wonders for the prevention of injuries as well as giving coaches a way to break down any technique in any sport into its component parts. By studying the mechanics of the human body in action, mostly through stop-action photography and slow-motion video, techniques could be analyzed, dissected, and segmented into smaller and smaller pieces. Coaches could then isolate the problem areas and correct any biomechanical errors. The idea being that by correcting the parts of a countermovement, you would simultaneously correct the whole countermovement.

Error detection and correction was a rational, scientific approach to improving an athlete's performance. It was also the athletic version of "linear system dynamics" which says: *the dynamics of the parts of a system determine the behavior of the whole system.* In sports that definition translates to *the dynamics of the parts of a countermovement determine the behavior of the whole countermovement.*

This was great stuff for tennis teachers. Correcting a player's crappy backhand was simply a matter of breaking the stroke down into its component parts, fixing the parts that were causing the problem, and voila! No more crappy backhand. Fix the parts and you fix the whole.

Linear dynamics coupled with sound biomechanics ruled the coaching roost back then just as it does today, only today the equipment is better, the data gathering is more precise, and the video is high definition and super slow-motion, allowing for even greater dissection of the whole into its component parts. We can now break down a crappy backhand into as many parts as we want, detect and correct any errone-ous parts and send our students back out onto the court with a newly crafted backhand built from error-free parts.

At least that's the theory. The reality isn't quite so rosy. Reality comes in when a student has to put all those corrected parts back together again into a corrected whole, and that's where the problems begin. You see, in sports, especially fast-moving ball sports, all those erroneous parts you just paid your pro an arm and a leg to correct have now got to be stitched back together into a functional whole. More exactly, you have to perform all the corrected parts of your countermovement in exactly the right amount of time relative to the movement of the ball or the behavior of the whole countermovement won't be the corrected behavior you paid an arm and a leg for.

That's the problem with a linear approach to sports performance. Anyone can learn the biomechanically sound techniques of their sport. Technique is all about performance in three-dimensional space. For instance, the three-dimensional techniques required to swing a base-ball bat are relatively easy to learn – and, in fact, should be learned if a player wants to develop as a hitter. But the real problem with a biome-chanically sound swing is that it has to be performed not only in three-dimensional space, but also in the fourth dimension of time. And that means all those biomechanically sound parts have to come together in the right amount of time to hit a fastball, the right amount of time to hit a change-up, and the right amount of time to hit a curve ball or a late-breaking slider. If you fail to put all the parts back together in the right amount of time, then sound biomechanics aren't going to raise your batting average one iota.

Better if the whole swing is performed in the right amount of time, even if the parts of the swing are somewhat faulty. For instance, if you successfully use your bat to keep an oncoming pitch from getting past your imaginary window, then the dynamics of the whole swing were completed in the correct amount of time relative to the Primary Contact Point, while at the same time, the behavior of the parts of the swing were completed in the correct amount of space – also relative to the Primary Contact Point. The parts of the swing might not be biomechanically sound, but the whole swing was perfectly timed to arrive at the perfect contact point in space and time.

Biomechanically, you can always take to the batting cages and practice your techniques. But on the day of the game, contact at the Primary Contact Point speaks for itself, and whether we're talking about baseball, softball, tennis, or any other fast-moving ball sport, positive contact always takes precedence over the biomechanical quality of the countermovement creating the contact. Positive contact is what ups your batting average, not the soundness of your technique.

This same scenario takes place with tennis players when they use their racquet to keep oncoming balls from getting past their imaginary window. Their whole stroke is completed in the right amount of time, while the parts of their stroke – no matter what they look like biomechanically – are completed in the right amount of space. In other words, *the dynamics of the whole swing determine the behavior of the parts of the swing.*

This is the perspective of *non-linear system dynamics*, and along with the Parallel Mode Process's radically different approach to the interior dimension of sport, it also takes a radically different approach to sport's exterior dimension. You see, non-linear system dynamics is the exact opposite of linear system dynamics. Listen to the difference: where linear system dynamics says: *the dynamics of the parts of the system determine the behavior of the whole system;* non-linear system dynamics changes everything around and says: *the dynamics of the whole system determine the behavior of the parts of the system.*

Translation to sport: fix the dynamics of the whole countermovement in time and you fix the behavior of the parts of the countermovement in space.

This concept, as you might imagine, was not appreciated in the bio-mechanically sound landscape that was coaching in the late 70's and early 80's. Even today, anyone who fails to kneel at the altar of sound biomechanics or dares to defy the tried-and-true dogma of linear system dynamics is considered too far outside the box to be taken seriously. But here are the facts: neither linear system dynamics nor sound biomechanics has come up with an answer to this one simple question: How do you play at your very best, how do get in the zone?

According to traditional coaching, if you can't get to it through sound biomechanics and linear system dynamics, then you can't get to it at all. So, get lost with your crazy non-linear approach to a linear game.

Of course, this absolutistic perspective is the very reason today's coaching methodologies can't come up with an answer to sport's most baffling mystery – how do you get in the zone? Traditional coaching simply takes the wrong fundamental approach to the co-creation of a unified performance reality. You can't create the zone through a linear approach that dissects unified reality into its component parts. Good luck trying to figure that one out!

You can, however, create the zone through a non-linear approach that goes about creating the dynamics of the "whole" unified state by shifting the whole operating system into its unified interior/exterior performance structure. That's the other thing I accidentally stumbled across in the summer of 1978 – a non-linear approach to creating the human peak performance state. An approach that doesn't say: change the parts to change the whole, but instead says: change the whole and you will simultaneously change the parts.

Here's how it works: by shifting the dynamics of your whole operating system from a Serial Mode to a Parallel Mode, you will also shift the behavior of the parts of your operating system from a serial interface to a parallel interface. In other words, when you shift your whole sensorimotor operating system to its Parallel Mode of operation, you literally shift the way it connects to the spatiotemporal dimensions of your R-field environment. Immediately, your whole system starts interfacing equally and simultaneously with the past and future spatiotemporal dimensions of your R-field environment thus creating the spatiotemporal dimension of the flowing present. In short, your whole operating system is *"in the present,"* and so are its parts!

Non-linear system dynamics says: the dynamics of the whole system determine the behavior of the parts of the system. The Parallel Mode Process says: shift your whole system into its unified performance structure (Integral Interior/Parallel Mode Exterior), and the behavior of the parts of your system will create a unified connection to the spatiotemporal dimension of the present. End result: flowing presence. The unified performance reality of the zone. You in your peak performance state. Or, you can spend a lifetime perfecting your techniques in an attempt to create the zone through sound biomechanics and linear system dynamics. Mind you, there is nothing wrong with sound biomechanics and good performance techniques, but you won't create the zone through perfecting the parts of your crappy backhand. Unified reality is a *whole experience*, and you only create a whole experience by connecting to the whole. And the only way your system can connect to the whole is by disconnecting it from the parts. The only way you can create a unified performance reality is by letting go of your serial connection to the parts of the environment in favor of a parallel connection to the whole of that same environment.

When you start connecting to the whole of the R-field environment while simultaneously observing its parts, you will soon find out that not only is the experience of this unified reality very different, so are you!

Moral of story: you don't have to be biomechanically sound to wake up!

Stabilizing the Zone

Getting into the zone happens immediately when you shift into a Parallel Mode of operation. Conversely, coming out of the zone happens just as immediately when you shift back into a Serial Mode of operation, and that sudden return to a Serial Mode occurs the moment you stop focusing on empty space and go back to focusing on form. In other words, you can come out of the zone just as immediately as you can get into the zone, and it all has to do with how you focus your eyes as the action of your sport arises in your visual field.

As I kept observing the zone from the inside, there were times when I would suddenly find myself back on the outside, back in my normal performance state. There I was, deeply in the zone, feeling the flow, one with the action on the court, one with the game, and then suddenly, without warning, it was gone. I was out of the zone, the flow was gone, the sense of oneness was gone, the connection the whole was lost, and so was my imaginary window. Once again, it was me against my opponent, me against the ball, me back in my normal performance state.

But just as there was a logical reason for shifting into the zone, I realized there was also a logical reason for shifting out of the zone. Every time I came out of the zone it was always accompanied by the loss of my fixed-focus state. Every time I stopped focusing on my contact zone and went back to focusing on the ball, or watching my opponent, or targeting the open areas of the court with my eyes, every time I went from FDF back to VDF, I immediately came out of a Parallel Mode of operation and returned to a Serial Mode, and with that return to a Serial Mode of operation came a return to my normal performance state.

And it happened instantly! As quickly as I would shift into the zone by focusing on my imaginary window, I found that I would just as quickly shift out of the zone by focusing on some piece of the action on the other side of my window. I didn't know what these sudden focal shifts were called, so instead of calling them "sudden focal shifts," I started calling them *"flash-outs."* Much easier to say plus that's exactly what they felt like. One moment I was focused on my imaginary window looking for the contact point along its surface, and then suddenly I would flash-out on my opponent's swing, or I would flash-out on the spin of the ball, or maybe the bounce of the ball or even an internal flash-out on my own technique or my shot selection. Some aspect of form would suddenly capture my attention and draw my focus away from empty space, and once I flashed-out on form, once I focally re-attached to form, I immediately lost my simultaneous awareness of empty space, and with that loss of awareness came a simultaneous loss of unified reality and a frustrating return to playing in the norm.

Flash-outs were difficult to identify at first because the sudden shift from FDF to VDF was subtle and happened unconsciously. But the more I practiced FDF, the easier it was to consciously catch these subtle flash-outs and identify their basic types. The most common were *pre-contact* flash-outs that occurred before I hit the ball, such as flashing-out on my opponent's technique to anticipate his next shot, or flashing-out on the ball as it came toward my imaginary window. Whatever the flash-out, it took me instantly out of FDF and put me back into VDF and with that shift came a simultaneous shift from a Parallel Mode and its integral consciousness back into a Serial Mode and its gross consciousness.

There were also *post-contact* flash-outs, most notably, flashing-out on the outcome of my contact, which, of course, took me immediately out of the process and attached me to the outcome – exactly the opposite of what Sport Psychology tells you to do if you want to stay in the zone! Stay in the process and stay out of the outcome, right? Except by focusing on the ball, post-contact, you immediately attach to the outcome, and with that exterior attachment comes its interior correlate in the form of judgment, analysis, excitement, disappointment, the whole spectrum of outcome-based emotions from agony to ecstasy. The point is, any flash-out on the outcome takes you out of the process, and in order to maintain the zone, you have to stay in the process, which means you have to stay in a fixed-focus state and let anything that happens post-contact remain out of focus. That's how you stay out of the outcome. Don't focus on it!

Easy to say. Hard to do.

As I deepened my practice of playing tennis in the zone, it became utterly obvious to me that getting in the zone was just the beginning. *Maintaining and stabilizing* the zone was the real heart of the Parallel Mode Process, and stabilizing the zone meant maintaining a Parallel Mode of operation with its concurrent state of integral consciousness. And stabilizing this unified performance structure meant one thing had to happen. I had to rid my game of these pesky pre and post-contact flash-outs.

I'm still working on it!

It's all about progress – not perfection, but when it comes to the co-creation of a unified performance reality, progress in the Parallel Mode Process includes a very real taste of perfection. The process not only gives you a taste of flowing presence, it also gives you a taste of who you really are. Remember, your Authentic Self only comes out to play in the present dimension, and flash-outs destroy your unified connection to the present because they attach your operating system dualistically to either the past or the future.

In the long run, getting to know your Authentic Self requires the maintenance and stabilization of the zone, which, in turn, means maintaining and stabilizing the unified reality of flowing presence. And that, just that, requires a symmetrical spatiotemporal connection to both past and future – equally and simultaneously – without any flash-outs.

That's quite a mouthful, but with practice, it is possible to create, maintain, and stabilize this symmetrically balanced connection to the unified reality that is the zone.

Competing In The Zone

Looking once again at Wilber's AQAL map of reality, you can see that not only does performance involve your individual subjective interior – your thoughts, feelings and states of consciousness (Upper Left quadrant), but performance also involves your individual objective exterior, your physiology, neurology and modes of operation (Upper Right quadrant).

You've also seen how you can shift into your peak performance state by changing your performance structure from this:

Gross Interior / Serial Mode Exterior = Normal Performance State

To this:

Integral Interior / Parallel Mode Exterior = Peak Performance State

But it is important to understand that your performance experiences, whether normal or peak, occur in a collective athletic environment that has both an interior perspective that is intersubjective and cultural (Lower Left quadrant) as well as an exterior perspective that is interobjective and social (Lower Right quadrant).

Briefly, the Lower Right quadrant involves the athletic environment of a sport. Take my sport for example – tennis. You don't play tennis in a vacuum. You need an athletic environment, a tennis court with a net and boundaries and fences and racquets and balls – all the artifacts necessary to play the game along with its rules and regulations. That's the Lower Right quadrant – the athletic environment with all its rules and tools.

INDIVIDUAL INTERIOR Subjective **(Intentional)** "I" Thoughts Feelings Intentions **(Conscious States)**	INDIVIDUAL EXTERIOR Objective **(Behavioral)** "It" Physiology Biology Neurology **(Operating Modes)**
COLLECTIVE INTERIOR Inter Subjective **(Cultural)** "We" Shared Meaning Mutual Understanding Relationships **(Competition)**	**COLLECTIVE EXTERIOR** Inter Subjective **(Social)** "Its" Rules and Tools Population Governance **(Athletic Environment)**

You also need another member of the tennis playing population across the net from you, a playing partner, an opponent, someone with whom you can hit the ball back and forth across the net, someone with whom the tennis experience can be shared – which brings in the inter-subjective perspective of the Lower Left quadrant – the game's shared interior perspective. The Lower Left quadrant involves the shared meaning of the game, the mutual understanding and communication that is inherent in the "we-space" that is shared in either a competitive or non-competitive format. Both formats have a mutual understanding of the relationship, and both formats have their own particular set of shared values.

A non-competitive format involves the mutual understanding that neither winning nor losing defines the relationship; rather the value set in a non-competitive format is defined by cooperation and development. Practice session, practice drills, even practice competitions are examples of a non-competitive "we-space" in which the shared values are grounded in the cooperation necessary for growth and development. The underlying reason for this cooperation is simple: no one is keeping score. Outcomes don't matter. They still happen, but no one is keeping tabs on whether they are positive or negative. Mistakes are permitted; indeed, mistakes are valued as learning opportunities. You learn from your mistakes. You fall down, you get up. You develop.

A competitive format, on the other hand, shares a completely different value set that is defined almost exclusively by outcomes – winning and losing. Outcomes matter when you start keeping score, especially in contact sequence sports like tennis where the results of contact are immediately realized. Your shot is either in or out. You either perpetuate the point with Positive Contact, or you end the point with Negative or No Contact. Outcomes matter, and when it's all about winning and losing, the playing *partners* of a non-competitive we-space suddenly become rival *opponents*, with one opponent essentially trying to beat the crap out of the other.

[handwritten note: ZEN / IT IS / AND / IT ISN'T ✳]

Modern athletic competition values winning, winning and more winning. Completely lost in the competitive mix, however, is the fact that we human beings have actually evolved to the point where we can come together in a relational we-space and share a mutual understanding of what we are doing there in the first place. When you think about it, that's incredible!

This intersubjective domain is not only a domain in which athletes share a mutual understanding of their competitive relationship, it is also a domain in which two very different competitive relationships can be shared. Both of these relationships are always available to us in every sport we play and in every culture in the world.

Imagine, if you will, a sport in which the individual athletes are

[handwritten note: ✳ ZERO SUM GAME / AND NOT]

competing in their normal performance state, a competition in which each athlete is connecting to the shared athletic environment in a Serial Mode of operation with its concurrent gross conscious state. This is Serial Mode competition, athletes competing in their normal performance structure: Gross Interior/Serial Mode Exterior.

What you get with Serial Mode competition is not only your least efficient operating mode, but you also get your gross conscious state, a state of consciousness in which the separate self comes out to play the game. It's ego competing against ego, you against your opponent, both of you wanting nothing more than to dominate the competition. Winner takes all. Loser gets nothing.

That's the mutual understanding in a competitive we-space of shared gross consciousness. It can get ugly. Emotions run rampant in the ups and downs of Serial Mode competition. Joy and despair do their dance. There are tears and laughter, self-hatred and pride. Emotional chaos is commonplace in the competitive we-space of shared gross consciousness. Two egos tearing away at each other's sense of self, using whatever means available to gain whatever advantage it takes to do one thing – to win. In the dualistic we-space of gross competition, winning defines the relationship.

Now imagine the same competitive we-space, only the individual athletes are competing in their peak performance state. Imagine a we-space in which each athlete is connecting to the shared athletic environment in a Parallel Mode of operation with its concurrent state of integral consciousness. Imagine a competition in which *everyone* is in their peak performance structure: Integral Interior/Parallel Mode Exterior

What you get in this peak performance scenario is a competitive we-space in which each individual athlete is competing as his/her Authentic Self. Each athlete is in a one-to-one relationship with the whole of the athletic environment. Each athlete is equally and simultaneously connected to the past and future of the arising R-field environment, each co-creating a state of flowing presence. Each athlete in a one-to-one relationship with the Whole. Right here, right now.

This is Parallel Mode competition, and in a competitive relationship, it doesn't get any better. Each athlete is fully present and fully aware of the action arising in its moment-to-moment dance. This is the shared we-space of *intersubjective unity* – a reality in which each athlete is in a state of integral consciousness, and this shared integral consciousness co-creates a unified intersubjective reality that is mutually shared at the same time it is mutually co-created.

Intersubjective unity is a potential reality in every competitive environment, everywhere on the planet. It just takes athletes who are willing to co-create its very special intersubjective we-space. You see, this intersubjective we-space of unified competition only comes to life when each athlete interfaces with and within the competitive we-space in a state of integral consciousness and a Parallel Mode of operation.

- Each athlete must do this: Integral Interior/Parallel Mode Exterior.
- Instead of this: Gross Interior/Serial Mode Exterior

These two competitive options, Serial and Parallel, are always available, already right here and right now. You can enter into your competitive environment in a Serial Mode of operation with its concurrent gross consciousness, in which case you will lock yourself into your normal performance state. Or, you can enter into the same competitive environment in a Parallel Mode of operation with its concurrent state of integral consciousness, and as long as you maintain this parallel interface, you will also maintain your peak performance state.

Understand, however, that these competitive options are mutually exclusive. You can't be in a Serial Mode of operation and simultaneously be in a state of integral consciousness. Integral consciousness requires parallel streams of information, equal and simultaneous streams of information from the past and future spatiotemporal dimensions of the arising R-field environment. That's how you create the spatiotemporal dimension of flowing presence, and a Serial Input pattern (VDF) does not provide parallel streams of information. Consequently, integral consciousness gets nixed when you're in a Serial Mode. What you get instead is a gross conscious state wherein the separate self-sense is firmly entrenched and wanting nothing more than to crush your opponent.

Conversely, you cannot be in a Parallel Mode of operation and simultaneously be in a gross conscious state. Gross consciousness correlates to the sequential stream of information created by VDF's serial attachment to the past dimension of the arising R-field environment. In other words, you can't be "in the present" (integral consciousness) when your brain is only receiving visual information about the past (gross consciousness).

Confusing, isn't it?

You still compete when you are in the zone, mind you, and you compete at your highest level. Competition is definitely included, but as you compete in a unified state, your normal sense of competition is transcended. Zone competition transcends and includes normal competition. Suddenly, winning doesn't matter anymore. Neither does losing. Playing is all that matters – only playing.

And when you are one with the game you are playing, you are also one with its parts. You are one with your opponent, one with the ball, one with the bat, one with the field or the court or the dance. There is no separation between you and the game. No division between movement and countermovement, object and subject. In zone competition there is only a one-to-one connection to the Whole. And with that connection comes the awakening of your Authentic Self. In the unified we-space of zone competition, *cooperation*, not winning, defines the relationship.

Flow and the Present Dimension

In psychology these optimal experiences are called "flow" experiences, and while flow experiences are not uncommon to sport, the traditional coaching community sticks to its belief that flow cannot be made to happen intentionally. The 'prevailing wisdom' is that you can only prepare for flow, you cannot create it. Again, according to the experts, flow happens by chance, not choice.

And again, with all due respect, that's just wrong.

Flow is *always* available to you because the present dimension is always available to you. The present dimension is always right here, always right now, and your operating system is *always and already* in the present dimension. *It's just not always connected to it.*

And it's not connected to the present dimension because your normal mode of operation, the Serial Mode, keeps you perpetually connected to the immediate past, perpetually connected to form. In essence, your Serial Mode of operation keeps you playing in the past and not in the present.

Nevertheless, flow is always accessible because your operating system always exists in the present moment. But because of the way a Serial Mode of operation interfaces asymmetrically with the past, your operating system itself is never directly connected to the present reality that is always right here, always right now. Flow simply will not happen while your operating system is asymmetrically connected to the past. It can't.

What you get when your operating system is connected to the past is your normal, dualistic performance state. You get what you always get; sometimes a little better; sometimes a little worse, but you never get performance outside the realm of the ordinary. When you're connected to the past, you never get flow. You never get the zone. You never get presence. What you get instead is frustrated. What you get instead is a sense of incompletion. Yet the notion of getting in the present can be misleading because you don't get in the present by thinking about the here and now or by paying closer attention to all the little things going on in your visual field. You get in the present by directly connecting to it through a parallel visual interface with both the immediate past and the immediate future of your currently arising R-field environment. That's how you create the unified reality of the flowing presence, and that, just that, is how you co-create the peak performance experience intentionally, consciously, by choice, not chance.

So rather than waiting around for flow to happen through some unconscious shift into presence, why not, instead, consciously connect to the spatiotemporal reality of the present dimension by consciously shifting to FDF? Once you make the parallel connection to your athletic environment, flow happens. Suddenly and immediately, you're in the zone.

Stabilizing this flow state, however, means maintaining a *continuous* parallel connection to the environment, and that's when the going gets tough. Only when the going gets tough in the realm of unified reality, the tough don't get going by getting tougher. The tough get going by maintaining a parallel exterior interface with and within the competitive R-field environment.

Doesn't sound very athletic, does it? When the going gets tough, the tough maintain a parallel exterior interface with and within the competitive R-field environment.

Sounds kinda geeky, but here's the truth: The reason it's tough to stay in the zone is that it's tough to maintain a parallel interface in the middle of all the chaos arising in your visual field. It's tough to stay defocused from all the action and stay focused on empty space. But in order to maintain the visual interface required to input parallel streams of information from the immediate past and immediate future dimensions of your arising R-field environment, you have to stay focused on empty space while form arises in its moment-to-moment advance.

That's when the going gets tough. But with the Parallel Mode Process, when the going gets tough, the tough get in the zone.

Opposites

Because we inherently connect to the world in a Serial Mode, we spend the majority of our time flip-flopping back and forth between the opposing spatiotemporal dimensions of past and future. We get caught up in "time's opposites" seldom unifying past and future to realize the transcendent reality of the present – a spatiotemporal reality that has no opposite.

Playing your sport in the zone is a way to transcend time's opposites. But in order to transcend the opposites of past and future, you have to include both in the co-creation of a unified present dimension. The Parallel Mode Process teaches you to create flow intentionally by connecting to flow's underlying spatiotemporal dimension – the present. Put simply, get in the present and you get in the zone.

That's how you do it. That's how you intentionally get in the zone – a unified reality in which form and empty space are no longer two; where past and future combine to co-create the present dimension – a unified spatiotemporal dimension that has no opposite. And as you perpetually create the zone through the perpetual creation of flowing presence, you get a taste of who you really are, a flicker of truth, a momentary dance in space and time with your Authentic Self.

Then POOF! Just like that, it's gone, and there you are, back in your normal performance state with its gross dualism and Serial Mode of operation. No more Parallel Mode, no more unified reality, no more playing in the zone. Back again to playing in the norm. Just like before. Just like always.

But something happened during your flow experience – if even for just a moment. Something very different, something radically profound. In that unified moment of flowing presence, everything changed. Your performance changed; you immediately played at a higher level than normal. Much higher. That's the obvious part. But you *felt* different, too. Much different. It was still you, but a different you, calmer, more focused, fully aware of everything that was happening in your visual field. For a moment in time, your awareness and your actions seamlessly merged. You played the game without thinking about playing the game. For a moment in time you were free from the nagging interior chatter and limiting self-consciousness that normally accompany your game. And the control – yes, yes, for a moment in time the control was there like never before. And there was even joy, the sheer joy of playing the game for no other reason than playing the game – right here, right now, in this very moment in time.

Question: who was playing that radically different game? Who was that profoundly different you? Who, exactly, was in the zone? Was it your egoic self, or was it your Authentic Self awakened and cut loose from the bondage of attachment and ego? And what was this radically different reality in which you danced the unified dance of oneness with the game? Why, in this transcendent reality, were you fully aware of everything while being fully focused on nothing?

Why the quiet? Why the calm? Why the lack of interior chatter? What happened to the voices that run roughshod over your mind, questioning and criticizing your every move? Where were the voices?

And the biggest question of all: why can't you play like this all the time? Why can't you always play your sport in the zone?

Actually – you can.

Once you realize that the zone is always there because the present dimension is always there, then all you have to do as an athlete is connect to that which is ever-present. To get in the zone, all you have to do is connect to the spatiotemporal dimension of the present, the now moment. It's always right here, always right now, and it always will be. You can count on it. Ever-present means just that. It's always there for you, and it will never *not* be there for you. But it's up to you to make the connection. But because we humans grow up connecting asymmetrically to the past and future dimension of our various environments, we never develop our capacity for making a symmetrical, parallel connection in those same environments. We never develop our ability to connect to form *and* empty space, past *and* future, equally *and* simultaneously. Thus, we play our games trapped inside the dualistic reality of our sport's limiting opposites while the freedom and fullness of our game's unified oneness passes us by unrealized and unfulfilled. Is it any wonder that we suffer in our sports? We're seldom, if ever, fully present to the games we play!

Fortunately, there is a different way to play our games, a different way that involves connecting to the perpetual dance of presence wherein we find the pure joy of playing the game for one, and only one reason – to play the game.

Right here, right now – always right here, always right now.

That's the zone, that's flow, that's the human peak performance state, and it's right in front of our eyes.

Patterns That Connect

Visualize these simple patterns: Throw and catch – catch and throw – back and forth – again and again. I throw – you catch. You throw – I catch.

Every father or mother who has played catch with his son or daughter has shared in these two fundamental patterns. Patterns that connect us to the games we play as well as patterns that connect us to each other as human beings.

The throw – a *Release Sequence* – followed by the catch – a *Contact Sequence*. These two fundamental sequences form the underlying patterns of the games we play. They are the *source patterns* that connect us to our games.

Contact Sequences (the catch in softball, the hit in tennis, the spike in volleyball) and Release Sequences (the pass in football, the shot in basketball, the pitch in baseball), both involve movement, countermovement, and contact, but in opposing ways. Contact Sequences involve movement and countermovement *coming together* at a common point in space and time – the Contact Point – while Release Sequences involve

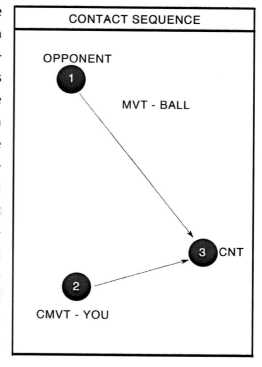

CONTACT SEQUENCE

OPPONENT

1

MVT - BALL

3 CNT

2

CMVT - YOU

movement and countermovement *coming apart* at a common point in space and time – the Release Point.

Exact opposites: in contact sequences, movement and counter-movement come together to create contact. The parts come together to create the whole. The many become one.

In Release Sequences, it's the exact opposite. Movement and Countermovement are unified, and at the Release Point (3) this uni-fied whole separates to create the individual parts – individual move-ment and individual countermovement. The whole divides to create the parts. At release, the one becomes many.

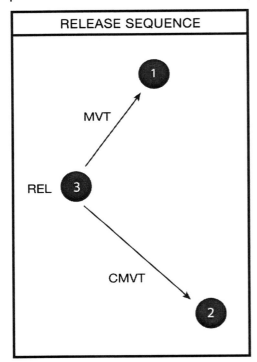

RELEASE SEQUENCE

1

MVT

REL 3

CMVT

2

Both sequences arise in space and time as *Relativity fields* (R-fields) with a past dimension *relative to you*, a present dimension *rela-tive to you*, and a future di-mension *relative to you*. As each R-field sequence arises in your sport, whether it's a Contact Sequence or a Release Sequence, you, as a sensorimotor operating sys-tem, are continuously inter-facing with and within the spatiotemporal reality of that arising R-field environment.

The Contact Sequence and the Release Sequence. Two simple patterns that create the foun-dational framework of every sport we play, yet the simplicity of these source patterns gets lost amidst the chaos and complexity of the tradi-tional approach to sport, which essentially says: *the better you understand the complexities of your sport, the better you will play your sport.*

Nowadays, it's all about complexity. And it all sounds very logical: the better you understand the complexities of your sport, the more accurately you will relate to those complexities.

Or so it would seem. The logic makes sense, but in the reality of fast-moving Contact and Release Sequence sports, a better understanding of your sport's complexities won't do you much good, especially when you're looking at a nasty curve ball coming right at your head, or you're shooting a free-throw to tie the game with no time left on the clock.

What you don't need now is a better understanding of the game's complexities. What you need now is simplicity. What you need right now is a one-to-one connection to the game's foundational framework, not a connection to the game's interwoven and ever-changing complexities. You need the big picture, not a bunch of little pictures. And in order to see the big picture, you have to defocus from all the little pictures arising in your awareness.

In order to see the source patterns of simplicity, you have to detach from the surface patterns of complexity.

Every day I watch athletes shifting out of their Serial Mode with its gross consciousness and into their Parallel Mode with its integral consciousness, and with that shift comes an immediate connection to the source pattern of their game that reveals itself in the sudden ease of their performance, as if the game had suddenly become simpler, less confusing, less complex.

The complexities of the game are still there, mind you. Form is still there, still arising, still ready to confuse the crap out of you if you connect to it. But when you shift into the zone, the ease with which you relate to form's tangled web of ever-changing complexities is not only noticeable to the casual observer, it is also immediately noticeable to you!

"When I'm in the zone, everything is so easy!"
"I can't believe it! This is so simple!"
"Everything feels so seamless!"

I hear comments like these all the time. But I also hear comments like these:

"I can't do it unless I think about it".
"I always forget to focus on my contact zone."
"I have to remember to focus on empty space instead of form."

Well, duh! Of course you do! That's the point! You have to be *mindful* of what you're doing with your focus amidst all the arising complexities, otherwise the complexities will take control of your focus and suddenly, there you are again, up to your eyeballs in befuddled confusion with too many things to think about and not enough time to think.

Example: You're the batter...a base hit wins the game.

The pitcher winds up...here comes the pitch...

What's going through your mind at this very moment in time? As the batter, how many different things are you thinking about right now?

Are you watching the pitcher's motion to anticipate the pitch? Are you looking for the pitcher's release point to see the rotation of the ball as it leaves the pitcher's hand? Are you thinking about your technique, your stride, your hip rotation, your swing?

Here comes the pitch...think about all the things you think about at this very moment in... THWACK!

Oops! Too late. Damn! The pitch is already in the catcher's mitt. Too much thinking and not enough time to think. Sorry...

Strike One!

Here comes the wind-up for the next pitch. What are you thinking about now? Your swing? Your technique? The pitcher's pitch? There's so much to think abou…THWACK!

Damn!

You were right in the middle of thinking about all the stuff you're coaches told you to think about if you want to be a good hitter.

Strike Two!

Uh, oh! Now you're in trouble. Two strikes, no balls, and the pitcher is staring you down with a confident smirk on his lips.

TIME OUT! TIME OUT! TIME OUT!

What do you need right here, right now? Do you need a better understanding of the game's complexities, or do you need a deeper connection to the game's source pattern?

Movement	→	Countermovement	→	Contact
The Pitch	→	The Swing	→	The Hit

Do you need to know what pitch he's going to throw? Do you need to know how fast he's going to throw it? Do you need to know if he's going to waste a pitch in the dirt or go for the outside corner? Maybe he'll go for the inside corner? Or maybe he'll come in high and tight, scare you with a little chin music…damn him!

What you're looking at is entirely too much information to process and entirely too little time for processing, and in this common competitive situation, a better understanding of the game's complexities is not going to help your performance. What *will* help your performance, however, is a better connection to the game's source pattern, and by shifting to your Parallel Mode of operation, you'll make the most efficient and accurate connection of all – a connection in which form and empty space are unified, in which past and future are equally and simultaneously included as you connect to that which is always already right here, right now, in your game, in my game, in every game – the presently arising moment.

Make that connection, connect to the immediacy of your game's presently arising moment, and that connection, just that, will improve your performance immediately by co-creating a one-to-one relationship with the game's source pattern:

Movement → Countermovement → Contact

TIME IN!

The pitcher winds up...what are you thinking about now?

Nothing...empty space...the contact zone... your imaginary window. And when the pitch arrives at a point along the surface of your window, your swing arrives at the same point. Nothing gets past your imaginary window! Ball meets bat at a common point in space and time ...CONTACT!

Movement → Countermovement → Contact

The source pattern of the game.

Think about that. Focus on that. Connect to its simplicity, connect to its truth, its goodness, its beauty, and you will connect to the heart and soul of your game.

Will you play better?

Absolutely.

That's the promise of presence. You will always play better when you play your game in the present. Always.

There's plenty of complexity out there in your sport, and if you choose to connect to your sport in a Serial Mode, then you'll get all the complexity you can handle. More than enough to keep you baffled and seeking for a very long time. Or, you can look beneath your sport's complexity and embrace the simple truth of all sport, the fundamental truth of all complex athletic environments. And the simple truth is this:

connect to your sport's present dimension and you will immediately per-
form at your highest level at that time and in that place.

The methods for creating positive contact in fast-moving spatiotemporal relationships can be complex or they can be simple. Presence
is simple. It's direct. It's immediate. But because it is so simple, present
moment awareness often appears simplistic to the complex world of
traditional coaching.

Well, here's a simple question for the complex world of traditional
coaching: is there a present dimension in your sport? Does right here,
right now exist in the games you play? Is there a present dimension to
which you can connect while all around you move the complexities of
your game's athletic environment?

The answer is always the same – a resounding "YES!" The present
dimension is always right here, always right now. Same place it always
is; same time as always. So if you're looking to solve a problem in your
crappy performance, or if you're looking to improve an already excellent
game, or if you're simply looking to develop, then making a one-to-one
connection to your game's flowing presence is a simple way to find exactly what you're looking for.

You just have to know where to look!

And if you keep snooping around in the complex world of form,
then you'll never find what you seek. For one thing, you're looking in the
wrong place. But more to the point, you're looking in the wrong time.

Playing a Different Game

You could also be looking for a little "self-transformation," an awakening to your Authentic Self, in which case, looking to the basic spatiotemporal patterns that connect you to the unified reality of your game is the simplest and most direct way to open the door to your own authenticity. Why beat around the bush? Why not go right to the source? Why not create the unified reality in which your Authentic Self is immediately awakened? Why not create the reality in which the *real you* comes out to play? Why not get right down to co-creating the flowing present?

Beats the heck out of trying to perfect the techniques you use to relate to the complexities of form. Connect to the present, awaken your Authentic Self, and suddenly, you begin playing a different game. Yes, you're still playing tennis, or baseball, or hockey, or golf, or whatever game you play, but you're playing it from a completely different perspective, a higher-order perspective that transcends and includes all the complexities of the game, yet simplifies the game through a one-to-one connection to the source pattern of all games.

That's really what you're doing when you shift into your Parallel Mode of operation. *You are fully connecting to the source pattern of the game with the full potential of your operating system.* This intentional shift to a Parallel Mode of operation takes you out of sequentially interfacing with the partial patterns of your game and puts you into a one-to-one interface with the source pattern itself. And that source R-field pattern is a pattern of simplicity that transcends and includes form's moment-to-moment patterns of complexity.

This shift to a Parallel Mode can be made consciously, intentionally. You don't have to wait around for flow to happen on its own – *for no*

DO WHAT THE
MOMENT DEMANDS...
CALLS FOR.

apparent reason. Remember, the shift to a unified exterior mode of operation brings with it a simultaneous shift to a unified interior state of consciousness – integral consciousness.

It is a shift of incredible substance.

Think about it. The intentional shift to a Parallel Mode of operation is an open invitation to experience unified, integral consciousness through the vehicle of sport!

And here's the best part: it's an open invitation! You don't have to be talented in your sport to experience your sport's unified reality. Nor do you have to be biomechanically sound or technically superior to awaken your Authentic Self. You just have to be willing to change. You have to be willing to grow and develop, and that means you have to let go of your normal subjective experience and awaken to a new subjective experience, a new self – your Authentic Self.

In the lingo of Developmental Psychology, it goes like this: The subject of the old becomes the object of the subject of the new.

Any transformational change involves the old subjective experience being seen objectively through the lens of the new subjective experience. You essentially look back on the "old you" from the perspective of the "new you." But in order for that "new you" to develop, you have to do one thing. You have to transcend the "old you."

And that's not an easy task. It requires practice. It requires discipline. It requires dedication and a willingness to go through hell before you realize heaven.

Primal Resistance

In his book *No Boundary*, Wilber refers to what he calls our "resistance to unity consciousness," (Wilber 131) with unity consciousness being the higher-order state of consciousness you experience when you are in the zone. Unity consciousness is integral consciousness, and our resistance to integral consciousness is a very real barricade to playing in the zone. When I first began training myself to get in the zone intentionally, I found myself slamming continuously, face-first, into the reality of this primal resistance.

It was a very real *interior* resistance that had an equally real *exterior* component. And that exterior component came in the form of my resistance to focusing on the empty space of my contact zone.

In other words, my interior resistance to integral consciousness had an exterior correlate: a simultaneous resistance to focusing on nothing. And as I trained myself to use FDF as my visual input pattern, as I trained myself daily to focus on the empty space of my contact zone and look for the Primary Contact Point, I found myself slowly surrendering any and all resistance I had to integral consciousness. By simply becoming more familiar with FDF, I found myself becoming more familiar with the integral consciousness that always accompanied focusing on empty space as form manifested in its moment-to-moment arrival on the scene.

I also started seeing flash-outs as symptoms of my own resistance to integral consciousness, whether they were flash-outs on the action in my visual field or flash-outs on the outcome of my own shots; it didn't matter. What mattered was the realization that every flash-out was a call to return to my normal way of focusing, to return to focusing on form. Every flash-out was a call to resist integral consciousness and return to the comfort zone of my gross conscious state. And once I realized my flash-outs were manifestations of this primal resistance, I was able to slowly free myself of any interior resistance I had to integral consciousness by freeing myself of the exterior flash-outs I encountered as I trained myself to use FDF as my visual input pattern.

Of course, it helped that FDF worked significantly better than VDF and that I played at a noticeably higher level every time I made the visual shift to focusing on empty space instead of focusing on form. Had I not played noticeably better when I shifted to FDF, had I not experienced the zone every time I shifted into my Parallel Mode of operation, I most certainly would have trashed the whole process right from the get go.

But it worked! It always worked! I always played better when I shifted from focusing on form to focusing on empty space. I always got in the zone. And so did my students. Always!

But here's a fact about playing in the zone. You will, as a human being, come face-to-face with your own primal resistance to integral consciousness. Over the years, I've watched athletes struggle to free themselves of this primal resistance to the zone's higher-order state of integral consciousness. We are so habituated to gross consciousness and its lock on the material dimension of form that any shift to a different state of consciousness is resisted at our very core. And yet the shift to integral consciousness is exactly that – a shift to an "other than normal" conscious state, a higher-order conscious state. And without knowing it, the unintentional shift to integral consciousness is exactly what happens every time athletes *unconsciously* shift into the zone – *for no apparent reason.*

Suddenly, they relax their conditioning to gross consciousness, and, in so doing, they stop resisting the integral consciousness that is always already there. And when they see their game minus any resistance to integral consciousness, when they experience themselves "in the zone," they also see what it's like to be free of the conditioned self who was doing all the resisting in the first place.

To be sure, that resistance is always there, but so is integral consciousness. Much of my teaching involves revealing this resistance by revealing its opposite: embrace. I teach athletes to embrace integral consciousness through playing their chosen sport in a Parallel Mode of operation – an operating mode in which they must overcome their resistance to focusing on empty space

Resistance revealed through embrace.

As you spend more time in the zone, you begin to see the different ways in which you resist the zone. Foremost of these is the call of our normal conscious state, the call of gross consciousness to return to the fold, to return to the comfort zone of normal consciousness and its Serial Mode connection to the material dimension of form.

That persistent call is always with us in our everyday lives; and it's always with us in the sports we play every day. It just seems *right* to watch the ball; it just feels *right* to connect to the action in our athletic environment by visually and mentally focusing on form.

But understand, a Serial Mode connection to the objects in your athletic environment is exactly what *separates* you from the action and makes the action exist "out there," when, in fact, it exists "in here" in your moment to moment awareness. And it is exactly this Serial Mode connection that imprisons us in our dualistic cage with its primal resistance to integral consciousness.

Two Pathways

Here's some basic visual neuroscience for those who think it's crazy to focus on empty space instead of focusing on form. My introduction to Neuroscience came in 2002 when I met Dr. Michael Mesches, a Denver neuroscientist, tennis player, and martial artist who helped explain one of the most ill-defined performance phenomena of flow: the fact that your response time seems significantly faster when you're in the zone than when you're in the norm.

Why is that? You're the same person. You have the same sensorimotor operating system. You're performing in the same R-field environment. So what are you doing differently when you're in the zone that would explain a response time estimated to be three to five times faster than your normal response time?

Let me repeat that.

Response times that are three to five times faster than your normal response times!

Imagine responding to the action in your sport three times faster than normal. That's huge! It doesn't matter what sport we're talking about, the faster your response time, the more time you have to perform your countermovements, and a countermovement that responds to movement three times faster than normal gives you more time to create positive contact .

I had always assumed this faster response time was a product of FDF, but that answer didn't cut it. There had to be something else, some deeper physiological reason why response times are significantly faster when athletes are in the zone. Mesches pointed to the brain's two cortical visual systems for the answer.

The generally accepted view in visual neuroscience is that the brain has evolved two visual pathways, one used for perception of objects, the other used for action relative to those objects. The *ventral* system, or "what" pathway, specializes in object identification, while the *dorsal* system, or "where or how" pathway, specializes in spatial localization of objects and action relative to those objects. *FINE CATCHES FLY*

The dorsal system is also called the "how" pathway because of its correlation to visually guided action in the environment; visually guided action such as hitting a tennis ball, catching a softball, or spiking a volleyball, all countermovements requiring a combination of object recognition (what/ventral) and visually guided action (where/how/ dorsal). *MOSTLY*

Mesches summarized the differences in how your visual system works when you are trying to "watch the ball" (VDF) versus how your visual system works when you are trying to locate the contact point on a fixed focal plane (FDF), and he explained it in a way that brought to life this very complex and confusing subject and made it accessible to those of us who don't speak the language of Neuroscience.

Here's a summary: when you focus on the ball, you are trying to keep the image of the ball on the center of your retina (the fovea) as the ball moves along its flight line. The fovea is the part of your retina that has the greatest number of photoreceptors and thus can discriminate the details of an object in your visual field. Watching the ball is a type of visual tracking called "smooth pursuit" and it works very well as long as the ball is moving slowly. But as the ball moves faster, your ability to keep the image of the ball on your fovea begins to break down, and at some point, the speed of the ball's movement makes it physically impossible to track the ball accurately using smooth pursuit tracking. Your eyes simply cannot move quickly enough.

When this break down occurs, your eyes make small jumping movements called *saccades* to reacquire the image of the ball on your fovea. We make thousands of these saccadic eye movements throughout the

✳ GREAT POINT

day, and while we are quite adept at them, they go by virtually unnoticed. We take for granted the way we use our eyes in our normal-paced visual environment because it's quite natural to use smooth pursuit and saccadic eye movements to identify and locate the moving objects in our slow-paced visual environment.

But in the accelerated environment of fast-moving ball sports such as tennis or baseball, not only does smooth pursuit tracking break down, but as the objects start moving faster, even saccadic eye movements can't keep up. So, in effect, no matter how you go about watching the ball in complex, fast-moving visual environments, you are attempting a visual task with ever-diminishing returns.

Sooner or later, your entire strategy for inputting complex visual information breaks down and your brain starts receiving inaccurate information. And with that inaccurate visual input comes inaccurate motor output. Inaccurate motor output that manifests itself as *negative timing*. *poor timing*

An analogy using two computers helps to clarify how these two visual pathways work. Imagine the flow of visual information that reaches your eyes as a giant highway. As the traffic on the highway moves toward an overpass, a video camera mounted on the overpass captures all the information and sends it via cables to two different computers – the *What Computer* and the *Where Computer*.

The What Computer is programmed to capture the details of each vehicle as it moves along the highway (e.g., Make, Model, Color, License Plate Number, etc.).

The Where Computer, however, is programmed for a completely different job – to capture the speed and direction of each vehicle as it moves along the highway.

For the What Computer to do its job, it collects large quantities of detailed information about each vehicle as it moves along the highway and then compares that information against a database of all vehicle makes and models. It makes these comparisons and measurements not only to determine the make, model, color, and license plate number of the moving vehicle, but also to note the location of the vehicle at different times as it moves along the highway.

The What Computer is specifically programmed for this detail-oriented task, and does it fairly quickly. In fact, the What Computer receives enough information on the changing locations of the moving vehicle that it can also determine *the speed and direction of the moving vehicle*, although it's not very efficient at this task.

The Where Computer, which is processing information at the same time, has a completely different job, and its job has nothing to do with the make, model, color, or other details of the vehicle. Instead, the Where Computer is programmed to do one job only – *to determine the speed and direction of the vehicle as it moves along the highway.* And to do its job, the Where Computer needs far less information than the What Computer. It only needs the information necessary to determine the time it takes for the vehicle to move from point A to point B and the distance between those two points.

Using this minimal amount of information, the Where Computer can accurately calculate the speed and direction of the moving vehicle, and because it only does one job, and because it needs far less information to do its job, *the Where Computer is much faster and more accurate than the What Computer at calculating the speed and direction of the moving vehicle.*

But there's another reason why the Where Computer is so much faster than the What Computer when it comes to calculating the speed and direction of the vehicles moving along the highway. Not only is the What Computer gathering and processing far more information than the Where Computer, but all of this detail-oriented information is being sent from the video camera to the What Computer over a *dial-up connection*, which, for those of us who can remember dial-up connecting, is very, very slow.

I NTENSITY AND RELEVANT IF TRUE

At the same time, however, the Where Computer is sending the minimal amount of information needed to calculate the vehicle's speed and direction over a *broad-band connection*, which, compared to dial-up, is very, very fast.

Input Patterns

So, what does this two-computer analogy have to do with response time and how you use your focus in a complex, fast-moving athletic environment?

Like the two-computer scenario, your visual system has these two visual pathways, ventral and dorsal, that are used to process the information that comes in through your eyes. The ventral or "what" pathway, like the What Computer, is designed to process fine detailed information, and it gets its information from the densely packed photoreceptors located in the fovea. This visual information is loaded with details, but the information itself moves along a relatively slow pathway to the visual cortex, where all the information is analyzed.

The dorsal or "where" pathway, like the Where Computer, *is designed to process and react to motion*. The dorsal pathway is also known as the *visually-guided movement pathway*, and instead of using the photoreceptors of your fovea to gather its information, the dorsal pathway uses photoreceptors that are scattered throughout the entire retina. The information in the dorsal pathway is not filled with detail-oriented information regarding the object, but instead, it carries information about the motion in your visual field, and this motion information moves along on a fast pathway to be analyzed in the visual cortex. ✻

When you are watching the ball or focusing on any of the action in your visual field (VDF), you are trying to keep the image of the ball on your fovea, which causes you to use the ventral pathway, and while the ventral pathway is very good at detecting details; it is not very good at detecting motion, which makes it the slower of the two visual pathways at determining the speed and direction of any moving object in your visual field.

✻ AND ELSEWHERE
C.6, PAMELA

Contrast focusing on the ball or the action (VDF) with locating the contact point on a fixed focal plane (FDF), a visual input pattern in which you use the pathway specifically designed to detect motion – the dorsal pathway. And while the dorsal pathway does not detect fine details like the ventral pathway, it is easily the _faster_ of the two visual pathways when it comes to determining the ball's speed and direction and _how to react to it._

Of importance is that both pathways are always active.

The ventral pathway is the predominant visual pathway used in the majority of our daily activities, and it's also the pathway we are taught to use when we begin playing tennis or baseball or softball or soccer. Coaches train us to "watch the ball," which means we are being trained in a visual task that is virtually impossible: the task of keeping the image of the ball on the center of our retina (the fovea) as it moves rapidly along its flight line.

We are also being trained to respond to the complex motion information in our visual field by using the slowest and least efficient (at least for processing motion) of our two visual pathways!

Right here is where the shift to FDF comes into the picture, because when you shift from focusing on the sequential parts of the action (VDF) to focusing on your contact zone and seeing all the action simultaneously (FDF), you are engaging the dorsal pathway of the brain, the pathway specifically designed to process and respond to the motion in your visual field - and to do so three to five times faster than the ventral pathway!

Sounds great, right? So why doesn't everybody just start using FDF as their visual input pattern in sports?

Here's why. In order to use your dorsal pathway, you have to stop focusing on form and start focusing on empty space, and that, right there, is where the battle with self begins. Defocusing from form is detaching from everything the ego needs to survive. So when you defocus from

MISLEADING
SoFT FOCUS
AVALUTP

form, you are effectively killing your Egoic Self in order to bring your Authentic Self to life.

The question you have to ask yourself is whether that trade-off is worth the effort it takes to learn how to use FDF as your visual input pattern?

Not only is the dorsal pathway faster than the ventral pathway, but the dorsal pathway also has a more direct connection to the premotor cortex, the region of the brain that feeds directly into the motor cortex, which controls your voluntary movements, which is another reason your motor response time is so much faster when you're in the zone.

Faster

According to Dr. Mesches: the speed at which information is conveyed along the dorsal pathway from the eyes to the brain is approximately 2.5 times faster than information conveyed along the ventral pathway. This *conduction velocity*, however, is not the whole story on why the dorsal pathway is so much faster. The route the information must travel to get to the part of the brain that processes motion is also critical

The pathway by which information travels from the eyes to the brain is fairly complex. It has relay stations, places where the information is repackaged and sent on its way, and substations where the information is processed, refined, and sent to the next substation.

Both visual pathways must first travel to a relay station before their information is passed down the line. Information in the ventral pathway leaves the relay station and travels to several substations before it gets to the part of the brain that processes motion. Information in the dorsal pathway, on the other hand, leaves the relay station and passes through fewer substations before it gets to the part of the brain that processes motion.

Moreover, the ventral pathway processes information serially. That is, information goes first to one part of the visual cortex, then the next, then the next, etc. The dorsal pathway, on the other hand, processes information in parallel, meaning the information moves simultaneously to the various parts of the visual cortex involved with assessing motion. This parallel mode of processing increases the processing speed tremendously.

Add all the facts together and there are three main reasons your response time is so much faster when you are in the zone. First, the visual information carried by the dorsal pathway is barreling along 2.5 times faster than the visual information carried by the ventral pathway.

Second, the dorsal pathway has about half as many substations through which visual information passes before it gets to the part of the brain that processes motion.

Third, the dorsal pathway processes its visual information in parallel.

- Faster conduction velocity.
- Fewer stops along the way to producing a motor response.
- Parallel processing.

Three reasons why your response time is so much faster when you are in the zone.

Engaging the Where pathway

[handwritten margin notes: "Fixed DEPTH of Focus", "What About No depth of Focus"]

Remember, both visual pathways are always active. The ventral or *what pathway*, however, usually predominates and is engaged every time you use VDF as your visual input pattern. In other words, when you focus on form, you are unconsciously selecting the *what pathway* to dominate the processing of visual information.

You can, however, purposely engage the dorsal or *where pathway* in order to improve your performance on the field of competition, and you do it by shifting to FDF as your visual input pattern. To do this you visualize an imaginary window spanning the court in front of you at a comfortable arm's distance from your body. Then, as your opponent hits the ball in your direction, or throws the ball in your direction, or kicks it, or spikes it, keep your visual focus on the window, and as you scan the surface of the window to locate the contact point, you will see the ball moving into clearer focus as it moves closer to your imaginary window.

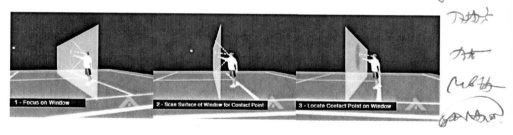

1 - Focus on Window | 2 - Scan Surface of Window for Contact Point | 3 - Locate Contact Point on Window

This is the FDF visual input pattern. With your focus fixed on your contact zone, the ball will be blurry until the last few feet as it approaches your contact zone. But, it will only be blurry to your what pathway. The where pathway, which only receives coarse information with respect to detail, will clearly track the speed and direction of the ball.

But beware, the verbal part of your brain will be screaming at you that focusing on your contact zone is crazy and that you can't possibly hit the ball, or catch the ball, or kick the ball, or block the shot, without first focusing on the ball as it moves along its flight line. According to the what pathway, *focusing on the ball is completely logical*. According to the where pathway, however, *focusing on the ball is complete nonsense*. The prevailing wisdom that tells you to focus on the ball involves using your most *inefficient* visual pathway, your what pathway, to track the movement of the ball.

But when you shift to using your where pathway to locate the contact point along the fixed focal plane of your contact zone, you have already determined the speed, spin, and direction of the ball before the what pathway even knows the ball is moving.

Question: is focusing on empty space worth the effort it takes to defocus from form?

IT'S A DIFFERENT KIND OF FOCUS

DO WHAT THE MOMENT DEMANDS

jp 5/25/24

Fiction or Fact

The Parallel Mode Process isn't shy. It's not quiet about its claim. It shouts from the rooftops that there is a better way. There is a different reality in which we can play our sports and even, with practice, live our lives. It is the unified reality of flowing presence. Not the past, not the future, but the equal and simultaneous integration of both. Right here, right now.

Consciously shift to your Parallel Mode and you will immediately create the unified performance reality of the zone, perhaps for the very first time, perhaps as another way to experience that which you already know. Either way, the Parallel Mode Process is just this: an invitation to transcend the ordinary, an invitation to experience your Authentic Self – and to experience it right now. No waiting around, no years of sitting in deep meditation, no then and there, just here and now. That's the zone. That's the claim. Do this and you will get that. Shift into your Parallel Mode of operation and you will play your chosen sport in the zone – immediately.

After all, why wait around to experience that which is already right here, always right now? The truth is that the present dimension exists wherever you are and it exists in whatever you are doing. The Parallel Mode Process simply invites you into the present dimension by showing you exactly how to connect to its exterior reality. And when you connect to the exterior reality of the present dimension, you simultaneously experience its interior domain – the domain of integral consciousness. Best of all, you get acquainted with the self who lives in that domain – your Authentic Self.

So the Parallel Mode Process is not only an open invitation to explore a higher-order domain of reality, it is also an open invitation to explore a higher-order you. And to explore this higher-order you, the Parallel Mode Process uses the vehicle of sport. Your sport, my sport, all sport. The present dimension exists in every sport, in every culture, in every corner of the world.

I use tennis because it is uniquely suited for connecting to, sustaining, and then stabilizing the unified reality of flowing presence. The repetitive nature of its contact sequence environment means that every few seconds you're involved in another contact sequence that begins with contact and ends with contact. The Omega Point (the end) of the old contact sequence is the Alpha Point (beginning) of the new contact sequence. Every few seconds, with every contact event, one R-field dies as another comes to life – again and again and again. Now and now and now.

The short duration and repetitive nature of these R-fields provides a perfect environment for getting into and maintaining the zone. And to verify your active connection to the present moment, a simple "yes/no" feedback does the trick. "Yes," if you keep the ball from getting past your imaginary window. "No," if you don't. Again and again, every few seconds, immediate verification of your presence at the moment of contact:

With that immediate verbal feedback comes the recognition of a one-to-one connection to the now moment, all the while maintaining a unified connection to the present dimension by maintaining an equal and simultaneous connection to the ball and your contact zone, to form and empty space, to past and future.

The Parallel Mode Process takes this simple yet direct approach to awakening your Authentic Self through a unified athletic practice that is easy to learn, sustainable, and fun! Let's not forget one very important fact about playing tennis (or any sport) in the zone: it's more fun than playing in the norm! And the more time you spend having fun in the zone, the more time you spend actively connecting to the present dimension, and included in that time spent actively connecting to the present dimension is time spent awakening to your Authentic Self.

Of importance is the fact that this radically direct approach to authenticity translates to other aspects of your life. The more familiar you become with your own true nature on the tennis court or on any other field of competition, the more you can take your Authentic Self with you when you walk off the court and into your everyday life.

Playing tennis in the zone awakens you to your Authentic Self through a game of "ball and stick" in which you actively create a unified sensorimotor interface that is immediate and verifiable. Pick up a racquet, visualize a window in front of you, and then use your racquet to keep every oncoming ball from breaking through your imaginary window.

Ball→Stick→Hit. Movement→Countermovement→Contact. The story of sport. The story of life. Writ large in the source patterns of Contact and Release.

If you already know how to connect to these source patterns, or if you already exist in the rarified spatiotemporal dimension of the flowing present, then you're already acquainted with your Authentic Self and you don't need this practice to show you the ropes. But if you're curious about your Authentic Self; if you're interested in experiencing your own true nature, or if you're just looking for a little self-actualization, then the Parallel Mode Process is an invitation to the surprise party of your life!

But you have to come to the party!

Of course, you can always stay inside your traditional box and continue to play your sport in your gross conscious state. That's completely up to you. For all you know, everything you've been reading in these pages might be total crap. This process might be a ruse. The notion of playing in the present might be nothing more than a clever temporal hoax. Playing in the zone might just be fiction and not fact.

But if you've ever lost track of time because you were totally absorbed in what you were doing – then FACT: you were "in the zone." If you have ever felt like everything came together for no apparent reason and you started playing your sport at a noticeably higher level, effort-lessly, unselfconsciously, with total focus and concentration – then FACT: you were "in the zone."

To call your experience of total absorption and flowing presence a fiction is to call the self who experienced that presence a fictitious self. In other words, you're calling your Authentic Self a fake, and you're call-ing your authentic experience a lie.

Was the immediacy of your improved performance a lie? Was play-ing in the zone a fictitious experience? Or was it real? Did you actually play the game at a higher level? Did you actually make a one-to-one connection to the game?

And who was it that lost track of time? Who was it that suddenly *and for no apparent reason* started playing the game at a noticeably higher level? Was it the old you who resists the integral consciousness of the zone? Or was it a newly awakened you, the higher-order you, you at your full-potential, your Authentic Self awakened to the unified reality of the present moment?

Was it fiction, or was it fact? Was the higher-order experience of playing in the zone real? Was the Authentic Self who experienced the present dimension real? Ask any athlete who has ever been in the zone if their experience was real and the answer is always yes. Extraordinary, of course, but also very real. Fact not fiction.

What about the self who was in the zone? Was that self real? Was that self a fiction, a false self, not the Authentic Self of authentic experi-ence? Which self is real? Which reality is real? If you've ever been in the zone, then you have experienced the unified reality of your sport. Is that reality a fiction or a fact? And if the unified reality of your peak perfor-mance state is a fact, then what does that say about the dualistic reality of your normal performance state?

Have you ever thought that maybe, just maybe, playing in the norm is the fiction and playing in the zone is the fact?

Ever wondered why you can't get in the zone every time you walk onto the field of competition? Why is that? After all, the zone is always there, the present is always right here, right now. So why can't you connect to the present moment every time you play the game?

Consider this: your Egoic Self cannot connect to the present moment because your ego is perpetually bouncing back and forth between a past gone by and a future yet to come. Temporal fictions both: neither is here, neither is now, neither is fact, both are fiction. Only the present moment is fact; only right here, only right now is there fact not fiction. Only in the present moment is there true reality, and only in the present moment can you connect to the full potential of who you really are.

Maybe, just maybe, the reason you can't get in the zone every time you enter the field of competition is that you keep choosing your Egoic Self to enter that field. You keep choosing fiction instead of fact. What would happen if you chose your Authentic Self instead? What would happen if you brought your Authentic Self onto the field of competition instead of your contracted, Egoic Self? How would you perform then? How would you play when your Authentic Self was connected to the fact of the present moment instead of your Egoic Self bouncing back and forth between the twin fictions of past and future?

What would your performance look like then? Would your experience be fiction or would it be a full-potential connection to the unified reality of your sport? On that day, at that time and in that space – would a full-potential connection to presence be fiction or fact? Is playing in the zone merely a great day on the field? Or might it be a taste of who you really are?

Question: Is flowing presence fiction or is it fact?

The Parallel Mode Process suggests that you answer these questions the only way they can be answered – through first-person experience. You have to experience the zone as fact to know the norm is fiction.

The House of Presence

One of the questions I'm often asked is whether the Parallel Mode Process can be taken off the field of competition and into the field of life?

The answer is yes.

At its heart, this practice is about playing in the present dimension. On the field of competition, presence is achieved by defocusing from form – the immediate past – and focusing on the empty space of your contact zone or release zone – the immediate future. This creates the unified spatiotemporal interface in which the past and future of each sequentially arising R-field are unified to continuously co-create the present dimension.

It is important to note that the unification of past and future destroys their existence as separate temporal opposites. In a Parallel Mode you immediately become free of time's opposites by unifying them in the co-creation of flowing presence. Past and future are no longer two. They no longer exist as separate temporal dimensions, and with the destruction of time past and time future you also destroy the temporal location of time's emotional baggage: past guilt and future fear, and when you destroy the temporal location of guilt and fear, neither can survive. What you create instead is a temporal location for the freedom and fullness of life that is your birthright as a human being.

The Parallel Mode Process shows you exactly how to co-create this uniquely liberating temporal location, and you co-create it by connecting to it, by interfacing with and within its temporal immediacy. After all, the present dimension is always with you, right here, right now, no matter what you are doing. You just need to connect to it. And when you connect to the present dimension of your current activity, you also connect to the present dimension underlying flow and flow's higher state of integral consciousness. No more resistance to integral consciousness, only integral consciousness itself.

Learning how to co-create this temporal location through playing your sport in a Parallel Mode is a way to immediately experience what it's like to be free from the bondage of time past and time future. Imagine the death of past and future through the birth of presence. This "temporal house" of freedom and fullness is the unified reality of flowing presence, and it is yours for the taking.

But there is a secret. You have to build this *house of presence* before you can live in it. In order to live a life of freedom, fullness and authenticity, a life that is free from the bondage of time's opposites, a life that awaits you in the house of presence, you have to first build the house itself, and that takes time and practice, and then more time and more practice.

This is where the Parallel Mode Process and sport can help. We know that to play your game in the zone is to play your game in the temporal present, and to maintain the zone you have to perpetually construct the present dimension by focusing on the immediate future of your contact or release zone while simultaneously seeing the immediate past of form arising in its moment-to-moment procession. Here's the temporal equation:

$$(\text{Time Past} + \text{Time Future}) = \text{Time Present}$$

That's the *Presence Equation*, and that's how you construct a very real house of temporal presence. The Parallel Mode Process is an architectural plan for constructing this house of presence, and with its construction, the house of presence becomes a living, breathing home in which your Authentic Self takes up residence. Think of the house of presence as the temporal home of the Real You.

And this house can only be built one way – *immediately.*

The construction, the living, the authenticity, all of it happens immediately when you move out of the domain of partial time and into the domain of all time: the domain of right here, right now – the domain of presence.

Learning how to construct this temporal house of presence is a matter of practice, discipline, letting go of self, dumping ego, focusing on your focus, being mindful of flash-outs and aware of the whole as the parts arise within its empty space. All-in-all, constructing the house of presence is not an easy build. In fact, it's a "rebuild." A completely new house with a completely new tenant! And the tenant is the Real You – your Authentic Self!

By maintaining a unified connection to the environment, either on the field or off, you are also maintaining the active construction of the house of presence along with the active life of its tenant – your awakened Authentic Self. It's not a bad way to live your life on the field of competition, and not a bad way to live your life off the field as well. You see, the house of presence is not restricted to sport. You can also maintain presence in your everyday life, in your work, in your relationships with people, places and things – a life of presence in which the bonds of past guilt and future fear are finally broken and you awaken to the freedom and fullness of your own true nature.

But, please, don't take my word for it. Go out and try the Parallel Mode Process in your chosen sport. Try it for yourself on the field of competition; experience presence in your sport by playing it in the zone. The Parallel Mode Process works for every sport because it's not about any sport. Rather, it's about the flowing present dimension in which all sports are played.

You will experience neither presence nor your Authentic Self as long as you play your game in a Serial Mode of operation with its dualistic interface. Your normal performance state is *not* the house of presence; it's the house of time's unruly opposites: past and future. It's the house of bondage, the house of ego, the house of self-will run riot. It's the house of attachment to form and duality, and as long as you remain attached to form, form wins, ego wins, your small self wins. Your Authentic Self loses. And your Authentic Self loses simply because it never comes out to play in the dualistic domain of time's opposites.

You'll never know what you're missing as long as you play the game in a serial interface. You can play the game very well, mind you. Good play one day, bad play the next. Good and bad live in the dualistic domain of opposites. Imagine what it would be like to play in a domain where good and bad are transcended, leaving only the performance of your Authentic Self, just that, just here, just now.

Imagine a full-potential performance free of good and bad, free of past and future, where form and empty space are not divided, rather they are unified. Imagine a performance where you, the subject, are not separated from the objects arising in your awareness, a performance where subject and object are not two. Where you are unified with the action, where you are unified with the game, where you are unified with your Authentic Self.

Imagine that, and know you *are* that. Right here, right now.

Contact Relationships

The state of consciousness you bring to the contact relationships of your favorite sport is generally the same state of consciousness you bring to the contact relationships of your daily life, and just as you can learn to shift into an integral state of consciousness on the field of competition, you can also learn to shift into an integral state of consciousness on the field of life.

Imagine going to work every day in your peak performance state! Imagine a state of integral consciousness in your job, in your relationship with co-workers or your boss, and if you happen to be the boss, then imagine relating to your employees in your peak performance state!

The source patterns of contact and release found in every sport are merely whipped-up versions of the same source patterns found in life, and by learning how to make a unified connection to the present dimension of these source patterns in sport, you can translate that same unified connection to the source patterns of any contact relationship in your life, and with this unified connection, your odds of making positive contact are raised. Just as presence raises the odds of making positive contact in sport, presence also raises the odds of making positive contact in life.

That seems utterly obvious, yet we are so habituated to connecting to the past dimension of our environment, so conditioned in our attachment to form, that we seldom experience the unified reality of the flowing present. Our gross waking state is mostly spent connecting to the surface patterns of form, which means we are *not* connected to the underlying source patterns that are always present. So instead of living our lives in the present, we live our lives slightly in the past, just a little bit behind the true reality of the present moment.

And we don't even know it!

It's easy to say that our relationships would be more successful if we were always "in the moment," but, as we all know, relationships are not that easy. Relationships are confusing; sometimes we succeed, sometimes we fail, but in many of our relationships, we're simply not in the moment. Mostly we flip-flop back and forth between time's opposing dimensions – past and future – spending very little time with and within time's one and only unified dimension – the present. Thus we are not symmetrically connected to the source patterns of the arising relationship, and that means our Authentic Self is absent from that relationship.

Ask yourself this: is your Authentic Self present in all your contact relationships? Are you always connected to the source patterns of the relationship? Remember, your Authentic Self cannot be present if you are asymmetrically connected to either the past or the future, but when you shift into a unified connection to the source patterns of the arising relationship, you also awaken your Authentic Self to that relationship, and just as your Authentic Self creates extraordinary experiences in the contact relationships of your sport, your Authentic Self also creates extraordinary experiences in the contact relationships of your life – whatever complexities might arise in the surface patterns of that relationship.

The surface patterns are always changing. Every relationship is filled with complexity, just like every sport is filled with complexity, and just as flashing-out on the surface complexities in your sport takes you out of the present dimension, flashing-out on the surface complexities of your relationships takes you out of the present as well. And when you become separated from the present dimension of any contact relationship, you become separated from its source patterns, and with that separation comes a separation from authenticity, from presence, from flow. In short, when you separate from the source, whether in sport or in life, you never get peak performance. You never get performance in the zone. What you get instead is performance in the norm. You get a relationship absent authenticity, a relationship filled with ego telling you you're right, they're wrong, it's not your fault, and they're to blame.

You get a relationship that looks more like rivalry than cooperation, and it all comes from an unconscious separation from the source patterns of the relationship itself. In the end, when you separate from the source patterns of any contact relationship, you get to have an inauthentic relationship with its surface complexities. In other words, you get a surface relationship rather than an authentic relationship.

Unfortunately, that's the norm.

A Different Perspective

When I first started playing tennis in the zone intentionally, it took a great deal of practice to get used to the difference in perspective that occurred whenever I shifted into my Parallel Mode of operation. For starters, I was no longer experiencing myself relative to the action; rather I began to experience myself *and* the action relative to the contact zone. In other words, not only was I aware of the action in my visual field as it related to my contact zone, but I was also aware of my own actions as they related to my contact zone.

I started experiencing the moment-to-moment arising of each successive R-field from a different perspective altogether – the perspective of the contact zone, the perspective of empty space – and from the perspective of empty space I could simultaneously observe object (the past movement of the ball) and subject (my own present countermovement) relative to the future empty space of the contact zone. Subject and object became simultaneous equals, no longer opposing each other, but arising together as one, not two.

This radical shift in perspective is part and parcel of the Parallel Mode Process. It occurs when you stop seeing the game from the perspective of self relative to form and start seeing your game from the perspective of self relative to empty space. Frankly, some people don't like it. They like the idea of playing at a higher level, but they balk at the idea of changing perspectives. They'd rather keep things just the way they are. They'd rather keep their normal perspective – self relative to form, self relative to the past – and in that conditional perspective, they expect to experience their peak performance state.

Sorry – that won't happen. You cannot experience the full potential of your peak performance state when a Serial Mode of operation limits your access to only half of the potential available to you in the athletic environment. Self relative to form is only half of the picture of each arising moment, and how can you expect to realize the full potential of your sport if you're only giving yourself access to half of its reality?

Obviously, you can't! Peak performance will never happen as long as you maintain the limited perspective of self relative to form. Refusing to change your perspective is refusing to engage your full-potential.

There are times, however, when you will shift unconsciously to a perspective of self relative to empty space, in which case, you will also shift into the zone, and while you enjoy the benefits of a more expansive and integrated perspective, you'll probably assume that the zone came over you for no apparent reason and you just had an incredibly good day.

You'd be right about one thing. You did, indeed, have an incredibly good day. But you had that incredibly good day because of the unconscious shift in your perspective. For no apparent reason, you stopped seeing the game from the perspective of form and started seeing the same game from the perspective of empty space. Only when you see the game from the perspective of empty space, it is no longer the same game, and your sensorimotor relationship to the game is no longer the same sensorimotor relationship. It is no longer a dualistic, asymmetrical relationship with only half of the R-field's full potential. It's now a unified, symmetrical relationship with the whole of the R-field's full potential.

What that co-creates is a relationship in which your sensorimotor operating system is operating in a one-to-one, unified interface with and within the full potential of your athletic environment.

Guess what? You're in the zone! And all it takes is a radically different perspective!

Awakening Your Authentic Self

Maybe you're already acquainted with your Authentic Self, maybe not. If you are, then you know what it takes to let go of your small self, your Egoic Self. Maybe you already know how to get in the zone. If so, then you already know how to connect to the flowing presence of your athletic environment.

Or, you might just think that your Egoic Self *is* your Authentic Self. In which case you would be wrong, even though you would be thoroughly convinced that you are right and all this talk of the existence of some mysterious Authentic Self residing in a house of presence is nothing more than a bunch of mystical woo-woo.

That's exactly how I felt in the late 1970's, before I started getting in the zone by choice, not chance. Back then, my Egoic Self was top dog. Any notion of a higher-order, Authentic Self was crap. The *Inner Game* was crap. Mental toughness was all about developing an impenetrable self-will, a powerful sense of self that could withstand the onslaughts of any and all competition. The zone was something that happened on its own, nobody could control it. If anything, it was the power of one's own self-will and mental fortitude that brought about the zone's peak performance state.

The whole concept of letting go of self was complete nonsense, and no self-assured professional athlete would ever think of trashing his/her self-will, especially a self-will that had been nurtured and strengthened through years of hard-core, Serial Mode practice. That was the norm in the late 1970's. Unfortunately, it's still the norm today, although an increasing number of athletes are realizing the limitations of their normal performance state and seeking out new strategies for peak performance, including new sensorimotor performance strategies. But, as far as I can tell, the Parallel Mode Process is the only Western process that suggests focusing on empty space instead of focusing on form in fast-moving athletic environments.

But as a practice, the Parallel Mode Process is not just about accessing the zone. That's a big part of its growing popularity with athletes from different sports. But it's also a practice that forces you to confront both your Egoic Self and your Authentic Self – and then you get to decide which self is the Real You.

Once you make that decision, you get to develop the self you choose. If you choose your contracted, Egoic Self, then you get to develop your ego. Just what we need in this world of millennial narcissism, right? But if you choose to expand and develop your Authentic Self, then you get to develop your own true nature as an athlete and as a human being, plus you get to watch yourself playing your sport in a state of flowing presence!

The Parallel Mode Process gives you a way to develop your Authentic Self through the vehicle of sport, your sport, played in your peak performance state, which is the only performance state in which your Authentic Self comes out to play. And as you develop your Authentic Self through playing in the zone, that same authenticity starts translating into your life. You start living your life in the flowing present, and with flowing presence comes a one-to-one relationship with life itself.

The Parallel Mode Process doesn't tell you *how* to play your sport, but it does awaken you to its authenticity. What you choose to do with that awakening is totally up to you. If nothing else, you will play your sport to your full-potential every time you get in the zone. Of course, every time you get in the zone, you'll also get a taste of who you really are!

You can't have one without the other, and with the Parallel Mode Process, there's no dodging the battle between your ego and your Authentic Self. If you want to perform to your full-potential, then you will have to put your ego in the back seat and wake up to your own true nature. Or, you can go on thinking that all this talk about playing in the zone, about presence and authenticity, about awakening to your own true nature and integral consciousness, all this talk about flow is nothing more than you having a great day on the field of competition.

Yes, it is that. Indeed, it is just that. The trick is waking up to just that. The Parallel Mode Process reveals the suchness of just that through the experience of sport, your sport, played to its full-potential by your Authentic Self, right here, right now.

No more. No less. Just that!

Potential and Creativity

Potential is defined as: existing in possibility; capable of development into actuality. In contact sequence sports such as tennis or baseball, lacrosse or soccer, visually focusing on your contact zone (FDF) involves intentionally focusing your eyes on the area of space and time wherein *all potential contact points* for the presently arising R-field exist in possibility. One of those contact points that exists in possibility will suddenly develop into actuality at the exact moment of contact. *QuinTAMESQUE*

Prior to its actuality, contact has the potential of being either *Positive Contact* or *Negative Contact*. It will be one or the other. A third potential, of course, is *No Contact*. You might miss a ground ball. You might miss a pass that was just outside your reach. You might miss blocking a shot on goal. Or you might fan on a late-breaking slider. Of these three contact potentials: Positive Contact, Negative Contact, or No Contact – one will become actual every time the object of contact enters your contact zone. *Focussing = Not Focussing*

Potential also implies the future: relating to a time yet to come; existing or occurring at a later time. When you focus on your contact zone, you are prefocusing on a time yet to come, a later time – the future. And in that future empty space there exists an event yet to come – contact. And contact will occur at a potential contact point located somewhere in the empty space that exists right in front of you, right now. In other words, relative to you as a sensorimotor system of countermovement, *the future exists right now, in the present, right in front of you, in the empty space of your contact zone.*

Co-existing with you in the moment-to-moment arising of your sport are both form (past) and empty space (future), the spatiotemporal opposites in which and with which your sensorimotor operating system

LET THE BALL COME TO YOUR STRIKE ZONE

must continuously interface. You co-exist with the past and the future, between actuality and potential, between that which is real and that which is possible. And this mixture of reality and possibility is found in every arising R-field relationship. It is a mixture that simultaneously contains what was, what is, and the potential of what can be. It is the very mixture of creativity itself.

Recall Whitehead's ultimate categories: The One, The Many, and Creativity, with creativity being *the creative advance into novelty*. Creativity can be seen in the source patterns of every sport on the planet – either the source pattern of the contact sequence or the source pattern of the release sequence.

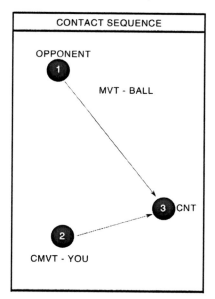 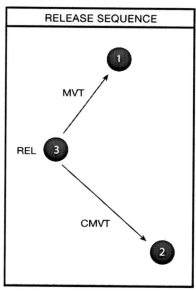

Both source patterns contain an underlying potential for creative advance, and with the birth of each new R-field comes more novelty, and with more novelty comes greater complexity. Take tennis for example. In every arising R-field in tennis we see the source pattern of creativity, and within this source pattern is found the empty space of the contact zone, wherein an infinite number of potential contact points exist.

MOVE IF you HAVE TO.

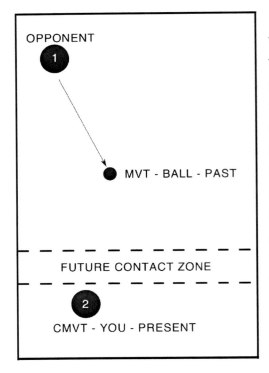

OPPONENT

1

MVT - BALL - PAST

FUTURE CONTACT ZONE

2

CMVT - YOU - PRESENT

Future points of contact where movement and countermovement will come together to create a completely new and different event of contact, and with that contact event comes the death of the old R-field and the birth of a completely new and different R-field, whose creative emergence perpetuates the life of the game itself. Thus, through the moment-to-moment experience of tennis, indeed of all sports, we come to experience the reality of Whitehead's "universal of universals" – creativity.

If you look closely at the ever-present contact zone, you will see that its empty space is the source from which all R-fields, positive or negative, spring into being. With FDF, you are asked to look closely at your contact zone, to literally fix your focus on your contact zone. But you're not just focusing on nothing. Instead, you are fixing your focus on the creative source of your game, the source of all potential contact. And with every new and different contact event comes the creative advance of your game into novelty and further complexity.

Tennis is a good example because contact at a 3-Point (positive contact) creates an R-field with its own set of spatiotemporal complexities; while contact at a 1-Point (negative contact) creates a completely different R-field with a completely different set of spatiotemporal complexities. The point being, there are different potentials existing in the source patterns of every R-field, and those different potentials allow for creativity to flourish and for novelty and complexity to abound in every emerging R-field.

In this empty space, new R-fields emerge, live their life, and come to their inevitable end at the contact point – the Omega Point that brings to completion the life of the present R-field – the point at which the many become one. But the contact point is not only the Omega Point of the completed R-field – the point at which the many become one; it is also the Alpha Point of the newly emerging R-field – the point at which the one becomes many.

The contact point is both Omega and Alpha; Alpha and Omega.

From the Omega perspective, the Many die to become the One. From the Alpha perspective, the One dies to become the Many.

All-in-all, there's a lot going on at the moment of contact! And for you to experience the depth and breadth of that exact moment of creative emergence when Omega becomes Alpha, when the past dies giving birth to the present, for you to experience the perfection of that transcendent moment in time, your authentic presence is required. The presence, that is, of your Authentic Self.

Authenticity aside, there are practical reasons for focusing on your contact zone. By fixing your focus on the empty space of your contact zone, your odds of being fully present at the exact moment of contact are greatly increased, and when you are fully present at the exact moment of contact, the possibility of positive contact becoming actual is also increased.

So it's not just empty space you're focusing on when you shift into your Parallel Mode of operation and start using FDF as your visual input pattern. You're actually shifting your focus to the source of your sport's very being, the creative source from which your sport *becomes* whatever you make of it at the contact point. Furthermore, when you intentionally make the Parallel Mode shift, it won't be your contracted,

Egoic Self interfacing with the surface complexities of form; it will be your expanded, Authentic Self interfacing with the creative source of your sport's very being.

What makes tennis a perfect sport for awakening to your Authentic Self is that each new contact sequence, each new R-field is created within seconds of its predecessor, and in those few seconds the creative act is culminated at the moment of contact. Then it happens again and again and again. With every new and different contact sequence, your own creative nature is awakened. Every time the ball goes back and forth across the net, you're looking straight into the face of creativity, and in that face is seen the very nature of the cosmos: the many, the one, and the creative advance into novelty.

If you are authentically present at contact, then you are witness to the creative advance that is the driving force of the cosmos. With every passing moment, in every emerging R-field of your game, you have a chance to create something new and different, whether that game is being played on the field of competition or off. We humans have evolved as systems of creative countermovement. We have evolved with and within the cosmos as the face of the cosmos, and that face is the very face of creativity.

Each of us *is* that face, and through playing our games in the freedom and fullness of our unified performance state, we see that creative face manifested in its most perfect human reflection. We call it playing in the zone, but at its deepest level, it is human beings reflecting the creative face of the cosmos. It is us, you and me, reflecting the very face of God.

Battling Narcissism

As you know by now, the Parallel Mode Process takes a very direct approach to letting go of ego. You drop your ego by defocusing from form and focusing on empty space. That's how you do it. You intentionally make the switch from VDF to FDF and, in so doing, you immediately detach from form, and when you detach from form, you stop feeding your ego the food it needs to stay alive. In a Parallel Mode of operation your ego is fundamentally dropped. And at the same time your ego drops, you simultaneously awaken your Authentic Self.

But in this era of rampant narcissism, it takes more than a convincing argument to get narcissists to dump their egos. It takes experiential proof. It takes a direct experience in which the Authentic Self proves that it can out-perform the Egoic Self. What better proof than playing your sport in the zone? Not only will your Authentic Self out-perform your Egoic Self, but you will also *look better doing it!*

Repeat: you will play better and you will look better when you shift into the zone. This tantalizing combination is tough to ignore – even for the biggest of egos. Remember, the reason you immediately play better is that your Parallel Mode is a more efficient and more accurate mode of sensorimotor operation, and that increase in efficiency and accuracy results in a higher level of performance. So you immediately play better when you get in the zone.

And you look better too! The closer your sensorimotor operating system relates to the action of your athletic environment, the better your performance looks, and the Parallel Mode Process shifts your sensorimotor operating system into a symmetrical, one-to-one relationship with the action of the arising R-field environment. One-to-one is the closest of all possible sensorimotor relationships. End result: you look better playing your sport when you are in the zone!

Oh, one small challenge. In order to co-create the one-to-one connection that makes you look better while you play better, you first have to get in the zone, and in order to get in the zone you first have to get rid of your ego. The point is, if you're the least bit interested in battling your narcissistic tendencies and awakening to your Authentic Self, then you might enjoy the Parallel Mode Process's approach to selflessness in which you get to play better and look better while transcending ego.

Best of all, waking up with the Parallel Mode Process is immediate. You don't need years of practice to awaken to your Authentic Self, nor does waking up need to be stationary and boring. Waking up can be active, and, are you ready for this – waking up can be fun!

Imagine having fun while awakening to your own true nature!

But something else happens when you're in the zone. Not only is getting in the zone a practice in which you *wake up*, it is also a practice in which your game *grows up*. In other words, when you're in the zone, you get to wake up and grow up at the same time!

The combination of waking up and growing up doesn't happen in your normal performance state. Your game will develop over time even if you continue to play in a Serial Mode of operation. Slowly-but-surely, your game will eventually grow up, but the rate of development you experience in your normal performance state is much slower than the rate of development you experience in your peak performance state. Whatever game you play, it will develop faster when you start playing it in the zone.

And even though your game will eventually *grow up* by playing in a Serial Mode of operation and a gross conscious state, your Authentic Self will never *wake up* while playing the game in a state of consciousness where ego rules the day. As long as you play your game in a gross conscious state, you won't wake up to your own true nature. For that awakening to occur, you need to leave your ego on the sidelines and start playing your sport in an egoless, selfless state. You have shift into a state of integral consciousness and start playing your sport in the zone.

Any practice that can shift you directly into a state of integral consciousness will also awaken you to your Authentic Self, so if you already have such a practice, then, by all means, stick with it. You already know how to get in the zone, and you're already acquainted with your Authentic Self. But if your practice leaves you unfulfilled and looking for that "something" that always seems to be missing, then you might want to try a more integrated approach such as the Parallel Mode Process

The very nature of the Parallel Mode Process is one of integrating the *whole athlete* with the *whole athletic environment*. And to accomplish this fully-integrated union of athlete and environment, the Parallel Mode Process suggests using a unified sensorimotor interface that connects you directly and immediately to the full-potential of your athletic environment, and with that full-potential connection comes a full-potential experience. Nothing is missing – except your Egoic Self, and in its place is your awakened, Authentic Self, playing the game the way you always knew you could play. You have found what you were looking for all along, although, all along, what you were looking for was never lost.

I suspect that if you are reading this book, then you've already had some experience with the zone, either in your sport or in your life, and it you *have* experienced the zone, then you have experienced the higher degree of efficiency and accuracy you get with a Parallel Mode of operation, and you've also experienced the selfless state that comes with integral consciousness. How you go about practicing this higher-order combination of interior and exterior integration is up to you, but remember, your Authentic Self only comes out to play in the authentic reality of flowing presence. Only in the immediacy of right here, right now will you experience who you really are, so any attempts at authenticity while in a Serial Mode will always fall short of full integration simply because you're operating system is not connected to the unified whole of authentic reality. It's only connected to the material half – the half you can see. And the half you can see is not the whole.

The whole environment includes both halves – material and non-material. The half you can see (form) and the half you cannot see (empty space). But the half you cannot see, the empty space half, only comes alive when you do one thing – when you focus on it. And when you focus on empty space with your eyes and your mind, that empty space becomes a living part of your reality, and with that awakening comes an expanded awareness of your environment, a more spacious awareness that integrates the whole of the environment with its parts as they simultaneously arise in their moment-to-moment advance.

This fully-integrated environment is your *Authentic Environment,* and it only reveals itself to your Authentic Self. Think of Peak Performance as *Authentic Performance.* And Authentic Performance that has two unique requirements: your Authentic Self interfacing with the Authentic Environment.

Authentic Self ←→ Authentic Environment

That translates to you in the flowing present; your Authentic Self connected in a unified interface to the Authentic Environment of your sport. Put those two together and you get the fully integrated experience of playing in the zone.

* * *

In the end, playing in the zone is as easy as fixing your focus on empty space or as hard as battling your ego. Authentic Performance is less about the sport you are performing and more about the Authentic Self who loves to come out and play in the Authentic Environment of the flowing present. The Parallel Mode Process teaches you how to create the present dimension in the games you play, whether they are games of contact or release. Whatever your game, presence is required to play it in the zone.

That requirement never goes away. You simply must detach from the past in order to create the spatiotemporal dimension of the present. How you go about detaching from the past is completely up to you. The Parallel Mode Process suggests detaching from the past by focally attaching to the future – the empty space of your contact or release zone. And while that might seem like shifting your attachment from one spatiotemporal dimension to another – and, in fact, it is – what you are actually doing is shifting your focal attachment from form to empty space, from something to nothing. No Thing. And yet, the whole time you are focally attached to no thing, you are still seeing everything just as it arises in its moment-to-moment procession.

You see everything while focusing on nothing.

That's flowing presence, and with flowing presence comes the awakening of authenticity: the Real You coming out to play the real game in a full-potential connection to the whole of your sport's unified reality. Not only will you grow your game authentically when you're in the zone, but you will also wake up as an authentic human being. That's what the Parallel Mode Process offers you through the vehicle of sport, your sport, any sport, anywhere, any time.

The Spiritual Dimension of Sport

The Parallel Mode Process is designed to give you immediate access to flow in the spatiotemporal domain of *relative presence*. But there is a higher (or deeper) level that co-exists with and within the domain of relative presence, and that higher level is the transcendent domain of *Absolute Presence* which also exists right here, also exists right now. It is the moment of timeless and eternal presence – absolute presence – that exists equally and simultaneously with and within the moment-to-moment arising of your sport.

Colin Bigelow, Senior Assistant to Ken Wilber and a developing tennis player defines the difference between relative presence and absolute presence this way:

> *Relative presence is being present in the here-and-now of a specific temporal segment, such as being present in the here-and-now of a specific contact sequence in tennis. Relative presence is being entirely present with the world of form as it is arising right now.*

> *Relative presence is what you get with the PMP, but relative presence is not the same as Absolute Presence. Relative presence is being unified with each moment of time as it arises sequentially, moment to moment to moment. Absolute Presence is being unified with Godhead, formless spirit, the Ground of All Being, ayin, dharmakaya, the Void, the Big Empty. Relative presence is unity with each moment of time as it sequentially unfolds. Absolute Presence is unity with the essence of reality prior to time itself.*

The Parallel Mode Process does not take you into the formless domain of absolute presence; it does not take you into the timeless and eternal present moment; it does not unify you with Godhead or the Ground of All Being; it does not bring you into the dimensionless domain of Spirit. The Parallel Mode Process does not claim to bring you into the spiritual dimension of sport; it just puts the spiritual dimension of sport right in your face.

Terminology is important here because the spiritual dimension exists simultaneously with and within the material dimension. We just don't pay any attention to it. And we certainly don't pay any attention to the spiritual dimension when we're caught up in the chaos and complexity of competition. And yet the absolute dimension of spirit exists right here, right now, with and within the relative dimension of sport. The timeless now exists in simultaneity with the temporal now. Think of it as the eternal now moment existing outside the spatiotemporal boundaries of every contact sequence yet also existing with and within every contact sequence exactly as it arises from one moment to the next. Eternity – right here, right now in the present moment of every sport, everywhere, always and always and always.

Absolute presence is eternal presence, timeless presence, but the notion of absolute presence doesn't exactly mesh with the traditional coaching dogma of modern sport. You're not going to hear a traditional hockey coach wax eloquent on the eternal present moment found deep in the heart of each and every slap-shot. That's just not going to happen.

But if eternity exists at all, then it must, by definition, exist right now. It must exist right here. How could it be otherwise? For eternity to exist at all, it must exist simultaneously with and within the moment-to-moment arising of our daily lives, including the present moment of every game we play.

At its deepest level, the Parallel Mode Process invites you to awaken to this eternal and absolute presence by first awakening to relative presence, and you can immediately awaken to relative presence by playing your sport in the zone, which puts you right square in the middle of the here and now. That's presence in the relative domain of your sport. That's your peak performance state; that's flow; that's the zone.

But here's the kicker: every time you co-create a state of flowing presence, not only are you spending quality-time with your Authentic Self, but if you look a little deeper, if you look into the very heart of the here and now, you will find that you are looking straight into the face of timeless eternity.

Contact Point Inquiry

If there is a single event that best manifests the present moment in the relative domain of sport, it is the event of contact; more exactly, the contact point itself. For example, at the contact point in tennis you will find the past movement of the ball, the present countermovement of your racquet, and the future potential of contact all coming together simultaneously at a single point that is both a point in space and a point in time –a *nondual* point in what Einstein called "spacetime."

The contact point is the one point in every contact sequence where the past, present, and future are totally unified in a definitive "now moment." The contact point is the uniquely singular moment in every contact sequence when you can be fully unified with the here and now of the relative domain.

But awareness of contact is awareness of something deeper. It is awareness of the exact point in nondual spacetime at which the old contact sequence ends and the new contact sequence begins. It is both the *Omega Point* of the past contact sequence and the *Alpha Point* of the presently arising contact sequence. It is truly a moment of unified presence in the relative domain of sport.

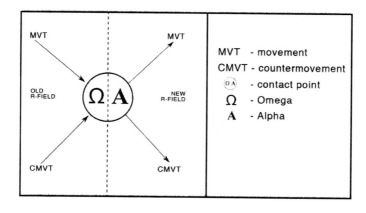

Nondual means simply "not two," and the contact point is a living example of nonduality in the relative world of not only tennis but of every other game involving contact. The contact point is nondual for several reasons:

- It is the point where movement and countermovement are not two - contact.
- It is the point where past and future are not two – the present.
- It is the point where form and empty space are not two – unified reality.
- And, when it comes to your sport, the contact point is the point where the game and you are not two. The point where you are one with the game.

Question: who are you when you are one with the game?

Who are you when you are no longer separate from the game you play? Who are you when you and the game are unified? Who are you when you are one with the moment-to-moment arising of each and every R-field experience?

The Parallel Mode Process puts you in the middle of this very special experience of oneness with your sport. And it is while you are in the middle of this experience of oneness that your Authentic Self comes alive. And that's who you are when you are one with the game. You are your Authentic Self.

But that's as far as the Parallel Mode Process can take you in your sport simply because your sport, my sport, all sports are played in the relative domain, and when you co-create a unified interface with the present dimension of your sport's moment-to-moment arising, then you immediately experience flow in your sport, and when you are play-ing your sport in a flow state, you are fully unified with its *relative pres-ence*. When you are one with the present dimension of your sport, you are one with the game. That's the zone, and that's as far as the Parallel Mode Process can take you.

But that's not the end of the story. When you are in the zone, when you are fully unified with presence in the relative domain of your sport, you also come face-to-face with presence in the absolute domain. The unified interface that co-creates relative presence in your sport is simultaneously the unified interface that reveals the absolute presence of eternity, so when you are in the zone, when you are one with the relative presence of your game, you are simultaneously one with the absolute presence of eternity. You just have to wake up to that reality.

The Parallel Mode Process brings you right to the boundary of this ultimate revelation, but only you can dissolve that boundary. Only you can see that there *is no boundary.* Only you can awaken to the fact that there is no separation between the relative domain of your sport and the absolute domain of spirit. There is no split between the material and the spiritual. There is no separation between the here and now of your sport and the here and now of eternity; no separation between playing in the relative presence of your game and playing in the absolute presence of God.

* * *

Shortly after I introduced Colin Bigelow to playing tennis in the zone (his first endeavor with any fast-moving ball sport), I also introduced him to hitting against the wall, a practice that can shift players into the zone as quickly as they can shift into their Parallel Mode of operation. In passing, I mentioned the "Thousand-Ball Club," a fictitious club whose members, however, are very real and have one achievement in common: each has hit a tennis ball against a wall continuously a thousand times – without missing!

Not an easy task.

When Colin first started hitting against the wall, I suggested a contact awareness drill in which he simply said "yes" at the exact moment of contact at his window, every time, again and again and again. I also asked him to report back to me on any zone experience he might have while hitting against the wall.

Two days later I get a call from Colin: "Three hundred!" Two days after that: "Five hundred!" Within a week: "I'm a member of the Thousand-Ball Club!"

When I asked him about his experience with the zone, contact point awareness, and the nonexistent boundary between relative and absolute presence, he wrote back with a note that he called "Contact Point Inquiry" and it goes like this:

Briefly, Contact Point Inquiry is a practice that relates to "Waking Up" and noticing absolute qualities while playing tennis in the zone. The most obvious practice that would fall under the heading of Contact Point Inquiry is instructing people to try and identify the exact moment when, with contact at your window, the old contact sequence ends and the new contact sequence begins. When, in time, exactly, does the Omega Point of the past contact sequence transform into the Alpha Point of the present contact sequence?

A quick visual aid with "O" as ball and ":" as strings.

At what exact moment does this: →→→**O:** *(Omega Point)*

turn to this? ←←← **O: (Alpha Point)**

When, <u>exactly</u>, does this change from Omega to Alpha occur? Tell me the exact moment the old contact sequence ends and the new contact sequence begins.

Can you say in words <u>exactly</u> when this happens?

If you had the world's most advanced slow-motion video recorder, would you be able to tell me <u>exactly</u> when this occurs? Would a machine that advanced be able to tell you <u>exactly</u> when this change happens, with absolute precision?

No, not with absolute precision, it can't. It can get very, very, very close, but it will never be able to tell you <u>exactly</u> the moment of this change.

You, however, exactly as you are, <u>can</u> tell me the answer if you know where to look, if you know how to look.

This is much like a Zen koan, because the correct answer cannot be fathomed in any way by the relative mind. Only by accessing one's own ever-present, Absolute Mind can one answer this question.

After reading this, I whole-heartedly welcomed Colin into the Thousand-Ball Club!

* * *

Over the years, I've taught thousands of people how to get in the zone, but, frankly, most players never go beyond the peak performance capacity of the zone. And that's fine! The zone is most definitely about peak performance in the relative domain of sport. Playing in the zone takes you to the very limits of your athletic potential while simultaneously introducing you to your Authentic Self, your higher-order, selfless self who lives in the house of presence. The peak performance experience, in and of itself, is extraordinary!

But playing in the zone takes place in the house of *relative presence*. It is an experience that occurs when you create presence in the relative domain of your sport. Yet at the same time you connect to presence in the relative domain, with no extra effort required from you, you are also connected to presence in the absolute domain – the domain of Spirit, the domain of God – you're just not claiming it. You're not claiming the reality of the spiritual dimension that is right there with you, already and always. Should you choose to investigate the domain of spirituality in sport, then contact point inquiry will put you in touch with Spirit.

Remember, the contact point is the point at which Omega and Alpha are not two. The contact point is the point at which the death of the old and the life of the new are not separate. The point at which creation occurs. It is at the contact point that we find the point of perpetuation, the point at which the game's moment-to-moment advance is seen when the information and energy of the old contact sequence passes seamlessly into the newly emerging contact sequence, and even as the old contact sequence dies, its information and energy are preserved in the birth of the new and different contact sequence.

In tennis, the data from the old contact sequence are included in the new contact sequence, and the creative addition of your own counter-movement adds novelty to the newly emerging contact sequence. All of this linkage between the old contact sequence and the newly emerging contact sequence occurs at the exact moment of contact in time and the exact point of contact in space. The nondual point in spacetime where and when Omega and Alpha are one.

At contact the life of the game is perpetuated logically and structurally from one R-field moment to the next, and with the emergence of every new R-field comes the creative advance into novelty, and thus the many become one and are increased by one.

Look deeply into that point. Inquire with your entire being into the very depths of that extraordinary spatiotemporal point, and answer this question: exactly when in time and where in space does Omega become Alpha?

When, exactly, in time does the old contact sequence end and the new contact sequence begin? Where, exactly, in space does the ball stop moving in one direction and start moving in another?

Slow it all down in your mind, and then slow it down even more until you come to the point at which everything stops and there is no motion at all, the point where the ball stops moving in one direction and *before* it starts moving in the other direction. Look deeply into the point where all motion stops, when all time stops, and you will come to the point of nothingness, the point of no motion, no time, and no space.

In this nothingness where there is no space and no time; in this dimensionless emptiness, Omega and Alpha merge into one. This is the point of Absolute Presence wherein you come face-to-face with emptiness. There is only nothingness, no-thing-ness, no space, no time, only the dimensionless void, only emptiness. Look deeply into that emptiness and you will see the absolute domain of Spirit. And here's the best part: *you are not separate from that.*

Question: who are you when you are not separate from Spirit? Who are you when you are not separate from God? Who are you when you are one with eternity, one with infinity? As you interface with the Absolute, you are your deepest self, your True Self. Call it your Eternal Self, your Ultimate Self, call it what you will, but know that this highest self is alive and well, and present in each arising moment of each and every contact sequence in your life.

As you play your sport in the zone, as you feel yourself becoming one with your game in the relative domain, in those moments of relative presence, you are not separate from the domain of Spirit. You are not separate from the eternal present moment that never changes. You are not separate from that which always was, always is, and always will be. You are not separate from Eternity.

Imagine that! Imagine yourself connecting to eternity every time you play your favorite sport! Imagine yourself interfacing with infinity every time you create contact. Every time you hit a tennis ball, or throw a softball, every time you shoot hoops or pitch horseshoes, every time you throw and catch or run and jump, you are a reflection of the ultimate categories of the universe. You are the many, you are the one, and you are the creative advance into novelty. You, right here, right now, are the very face of God.

Is there a spiritual dimension to sport? Play your game in the zone and find out. Use the Parallel Mode Process to become one with your game in the relative domain of flowing presence. Then inquire deeply into your game's point of contact, its point of release, its point of perpetuation, inquire into the very heart of your game's unified nature, where Omega and Alpha are not two, where relative and absolute are not two, where form and emptiness are no longer separate domains but merge into ultimate unified reality. Get to know your Authentic Self by playing your sport in the zone and then awaken to your Eternal Self through inquiring into that which is found at the heart of every contact point, at the very moment of creation when the many become one and are increased by one.

Question: Who are you at that moment of Absolute and Eternal presence? Who are you when you are one with Spirit?

Go For The Zone

The primary calling card of the Parallel Mode Process has always been peak performance, playing your sport in the zone. On a deeper level the zone is a call to authenticity, awakening to your Authentic Self. And at its deepest level this practice is a call to spiritual embrace, an inquiry into Alpha and Omega, wherein the veil of relative time is lifted to reveal Eternity.

The Parallel Mode Process invites you to experience the zone at any or all of these levels. And, remember, you don't have to be a world-class athlete to get in the zone; you just have to be willing to make some changes in how you interface with your athletic environment. Mostly, you have to be willing to investigate the reality of your Authentic Self, and to investigate that higher-order reality, all you have to do is shift into your Parallel Mode.

Do that – make the shift to your Parallel Mode – and you will immediately start playing in the zone! It is a shift of radical significance – a shift into a higher-order performance state created by a higher-order you. That's the zone. Your sport is just the vehicle for making the shift, and it's the same shift for all athletes in all sports, whether it's baseball, tennis, golf, volleyball, soccer, or lacrosse. The sport doesn't matter. The shift does. And the shift is not only a shift from Serial to Parallel operation; it is also a shift from gross to integral consciousness. Both are required to access the zone.

So in the end, the question is this: how do *you* make the shift? How do *you* access the zone? There are two fundamental approaches. You can take the interior approach and access the zone through a shift from gross to integral consciousness, or you can take the exterior approach and access the zone through a shift from Serial to Parallel operation.

The interior approach for accessing the zone through a controlled shift in conscious states can take years of meditation and contemplative practice before you get any results, and while there is nothing wrong with the interior approach, who wants to wait for years to get in the zone?

But when you make the exterior shift to a Parallel Mode of operation, you access the zone immediately. In minutes – not years! And here's the best part: once you learn how to shift from Serial to Parallel operation, not only will you start accessing your most efficient and accurate mode of exterior operation, you will also start accessing its corresponding state of interior consciousness – integral consciousness. Put them together and you get the zone –immediately.

It takes a radically different approach to create this radically different experience of the zone, and you're not going to find anything radically different in the hallowed halls of traditional coaching. Ask a traditional coach how to get in the zone, or, better yet, ask a traditional coach how to access integral consciousness, and you'll get a befuddled look that says, "Huh? What the hell are you talking about? You don't need to access anything but better biomechanics, pal! That's what you need! All this crap about higher consciousness and playing in the zone is nothing but talk. If you're looking for all that woo-woo stuff, then go someplace else!"

Exactly! Go someplace else. When it comes to playing in the zone, that's the best advice you will get from the traditional coaching community – *go someplace else!* You're not going to learn how to access the zone from a coach who thinks the zone is woo-woo. You have to look elsewhere. Find a different coach, find a different practice, one that not only sees the zone as a reality, but practices accessing that reality on a daily basis. Find a practice where it's not about the game being played, but about the consciousness of the player. A practice that asks the fundamental question: *who, exactly, is playing the game?*

Who, exactly, is playing your sport when you step onto the field of competition? Is it your Egoic Self playing the game in your gross conscious state and a Serial Mode of operation? Or is it your Authentic Self playing the game in a Parallel Mode of Operation with its corresponding state of integral consciousness?

If it's the former, you will never experience the zone. Your performance structure (Gross Interior/Serial Exterior) locks you into your normal performance state while locking you out of the zone. If it's the latter, you will always experience the zone. Your performance structure (Integral Interior/Parallel Exterior) transcends your normal performance state and gives you immediate access to the zone.

Remember, the traditional approach to peak performance deals with improving your biomechanics, and while improving your biomechanics will certainly improve your performance, *it will not get you in the zone!* What gets you in the zone is a shift in the whole of your performance structure – both its interior state of consciousness and its exterior mode of operation. Improving your biomechanics addresses neither. It just makes you look good on the outside.

Unfortunately, sound biomechanics on the outside doesn't change your conscious state on the inside, nor does it change the way your operating system interfaces with the spatiotemporal complexities of any fast-moving, R-field environment. You can possess perfectly sound biomechanics, but if you continue to interface with the complexities of your R-field environment in a Serial Mode of operation, then your perfectly sound biomechanics will continue to be performed in a state of gross consciousness. In other words, your game will be biomechanically sound, but you'll be playing it in the norm – not in the zone.

That's as far as traditional coaching can take you: a biomechanically sound game played in your normal performance state. And while there is nothing wrong with that performance scenario, it is not the performance scenario for playing your game in the zone. Of course, you can always settle for playing in the norm. Most people do. Most people would rather look good playing in their normal performance state than risk letting go of their ego to experience the zone.

Your ego will tell you with the clearest of rational convictions that the road to peak performance is paved with sound biomechanics; all this talk about playing in the zone is a bunch of crap. Meanwhile, there are plenty of traditional coaches out there in the athletic world who are very adept at the biomechanics of your game. In fact, they're every-where – and they're very good at what they do! So if your goal is to get better at your biomechanics, then you won't have any trouble finding a coach to help you improve your game without threatening your ego.

But if you're looking for something different, something deeper, if you're looking for a way to transcend the norm and experience higher-order consciousness and peak performance, then you won't find it in the traditional coaching community. You will, however, find it in a small but growing community of integrally-informed coaches and teachers whose instruction includes both exterior performance *and* interior con-sciousness. Coaches who don't dodge the interior component of sport, but rather embrace it, teach it, and practice it themselves.

These are the coaches to contact if you want to take yourself and your sport into the full-potential of your physical, mental, and spiritual capacities. And all you have to do to identify one of these integrally-informed coaches is ask them a simple question: how do I play my sport "in the zone?"

If they look at you funny and start beating around the bush, talking high-performance techniques and kinetic chains and strategic devel-opment, then you're looking at another traditional coach. But if, at the very mention of playing in the zone, their eyes light up and they start talking about quadrants and correlations, interiors and exteriors, focus and flow, mind, body and spirit; if they talk about the player and not the game, then you've found something very special. You've found a home in which to develop both your game as an athlete and your authenticity as a human being. You've found a place where you can grow up and wake up at the same time.

Go for it! Go for the zone!

Afterword

By Colin Bigelow

The Parallel Mode Process helped me at a time in my life when nothing else could. In the Spring of 2010 I was in a state of profound internal division, and I was having tremendous difficulty integrating my experience. I had had several very deep experiences of my own True Self, the Absolutely Identity in each one of us that is timeless, limitless, and formless, and I had seen that this True Self was in fact identical with the entire world of form. The Buddhists like to say that nirvana and samsara are nondual, and I had been introduced to this understanding in such a way that I was henceforth *certain* that it was true: my own deepest identity is infinite and eternal, and this Empty Ground of Being that I AM is creating the entire universe moment-to-moment. The taste of Freedom and the taste of Form were the same taste—One Taste.

The problem was, One Taste was not what I actually experienced most of the time. What I actually experienced most of the time was a reality fundamentally split in two, with the infinite on one side and the finite on the other. I knew in an unshakeable way that my true identity—and the true nature of reality—was composed of both infinite and finite qualities perfectly, easily, and spontaneously co-arising in Divine harmony. Again, what I actually experienced 99% of the time was nothing like this. I could intuit my own Formless identity at nearly all times, which is generally a good thing, but the way this Empty identity *felt* was profoundly divorced and dissociated from my actual human life. I could be the formless Witness of my life, but I could never touch it, integrate it, unify it. I was *certain* my own spiritual heart was composed of two lovers united as one, the unmanifest and the manifest in supreme embrace, but although I could perceive both at the same time, they felt quite literally worlds apart. Nothing could shake me of my conviction that reality was utterly nondual, and yet all I experienced for several years was rather extreme and painful duality. And then I met Scott.

Scott came to meet with Ken in May 2010, and I sat in on the meeting. Scott was telling Ken that he had developed a technique whereby anyone capable of holding a tennis racquet would almost instantly get into "the zone." The zone, Scott explained, was the Holy Grail of athletic peak performance, whereby athletes consistently reported a near total loss of self-awareness, resulting in a unity or integral state of consciousness whereby they felt "one" with *everything* in their environment. It is said that their action and awareness merge, such that there is no difference whatsoever between intending a movement and its execution; it is said that it *feels* like there is no separation whatsoever between you, your actions, and everything arising in that moment. Boy, did I love the sound of that. It sounded very similar to what I had experienced in my own spontaneous nondual states, so I volunteered to join Scott on-court for an introductory lesson.

I should explain that one of the primary features of my experience at that time was the inability to enjoy much of anything. I felt very much like a disembodied eyeball hovering 5'10" above the ground with a body dangling off of it. Like I said, I could Witness my life but never touch it. I was the Empty Observer, and it didn't appear that anything whatsoever had the ability to break through the glass wall separating me from my life. It was as if I lived behind a three-inch thick piece of bulletproof glass, the kind bank tellers and prisoners sit behind—and in this metaphor, I was without question a prisoner. Everything in my life was crystal clear and high-resolution, I just couldn't touch it. It was like smearing a frosted cupcake against one side of the glass and then desperately licking at it from the other side—it just doesn't work. It was incredibly frustrating and utterly unsatisfying. This was my life.

So in this context, it's no small thing to say that the first thing I noticed about Scott's practice was that it was *fun*. It also turned out to be incredibly appropriate that I felt like I lived behind a sheet of impenetrable glass, because Scott's practice consisted of exactly one instruction: use your racquet to keep the ball from getting past an imaginary window a comfortable arm's length in front of you. That was it. So I did what Scott told me, and almost immediately I was enjoying myself—a lot! This was *very* interesting, because before Scott gave me his imaginary window instruction he had me simply try and "hit the ball" back to him, with no pointers on how to do so at all. I think I missed the first ball, the second ball hit the frame of my racquet and shot towards the ceiling, and the third ball went into the net. This wasn't so much fun— and why the hell do I care about this anyway? I'm interested in Enlightened awareness, not my ability to hit fuzzy yellow balls over some net.

But like I said, as soon as Scott told me to "defend my imaginary window" with my racquet, I immediately started having fun. For one thing, I started being able to hit most of the balls back to him, so I didn't feel quite so ridiculous out on a tennis court. I did track, swimming, and cross country skiing in high school, but I had no training whatsoever in any sport that involved a moving object, and I was *not* naturally gifted in terms of hand-eye coordination. For everyone else at the courts that day, it was obvious I had no clue what to do with a tennis racquet in my hand, and the five-year-olds a few yards over were putting me to shame. Scott told me not to worry about any of this, and to simply keep the ball from getting past my window. What did I have to lose? I certainly couldn't get any worse. So I did what he said, and by golly I started getting most of the balls back to him. Neat!

Before I knew it, an hour and a half had gone by, and I couldn't seem to stop smiling. I truly could not remember the last time I had had this much fun. This feels so familiar, so easy, so natural, I kept thinking to my-self… when have I felt this way before? That's when I realized I didn't feel separate. The most profound nondual satori I had ever experienced was during a walk in the mountains, and that's what this felt like. The experi-ence in the mountains was spontaneous; it came, it blew my mind, and it went. But what I had just done here with Scott was an actual *practice*, something I could repeat. I couldn't help but wonder: if I do this practice again, will I feel this way again—or was it a fluke?

It wasn't a fluke. Scott kept inviting me to deepen my experience with his practice, and I kept feeling the bulletproof glass that kept me miles away from my life dissolve. I was enjoying myself, I was smiling, I was *happy*. This was nothing short of a revelation for me. I had spent *years* trying to collapse the Grand Canyon between subject and object with limited success. Nothing helped the Witness give up the ghost and dissolve into the universe I could actually touch. Nothing except… tennis?

It's worth mentioning here that I have had a somewhat unusual rela-tionship with spiritual "practice." Ever since I was 15 or so, the time of my first kensho, I have had the unshakable knowledge, conviction, and in-tuition that ultimate Reality is ever-present, even if it was not what I was experiencing. Therefore, I spent very little of my time or energy "seeking out" spiritual practices to discover that which I knew to be ever-present. I felt that most spiritual practices were forms of seeking—indeed, for most people that is exactly what they are—and so I simply never stuck with any formal spiritual practices beyond the introductory stages. Part of why I was able to stick with Scott's practice is that, well, it's tennis. It's a *game* for goodness sake; it's as secular as you can get. My normal anti-bodies for *spiritual* practice were never activated, and therefore it never felt like I was actively *seeking* ever-present Spirit.

My spiritual understanding and orientation as a whole is nearly entirely the result of my twelve years working with Ken Wilber day in and day out, and having his guidance always available to me as a friend and mentor. However, because Ken is a *pandit* (an awakened scholar who does not take on students, rather than a *guru*, who does) Ken never actually *assigned* me any practices. He recommended to me what he recommends in his books to everyone else, namely: develop the most comprehensive Integral Life Practice you can, and part of that is—ideally—developing a relationship with a teacher who *does* specialize in "pointing out" ever-present Spirit, and will personally walk you through that process. Combined with my proclivity to *not do* spiritual practice, I never ended up studying with specifically spiritual teachers, or doing the practice they recommended, in a terribly consistent manner. (That said, I did study with Andrew Cohen for two years and with Genpo Roshi for several retreats, and I would recommend both of them very highly.)

My work with Ken had opened me to repeated direct experiences of nondual Spirit. Equally important—and, if you can imagine, perhaps even *more* important—Ken had taught me how to *interpret* Spirit in the fullest possible manner (the *Emptiness* of Enlightenment is the same for all individuals throughout time; the *Fullness* of Enlightenment is subject to evolution—see *Integral Spirituality*). It was true however that I was lacking in consistent spiritual practice of a certain kind, and although I was aggravatingly *close* to a steady realization of my own True Self, I was having trouble stabilizing what I *knew* to be Real in every moment. This is part of the genius of Scott's practice: you end up doing spiritual work—accessing states of consciousness—within a low-pressure, not overtly-spiritual context, and when you *stop seeking* Spirit, there is finally the space to notice it. Combined with everything I had learned from Ken, this was most certainly my experience. Scott Ford got me to do spiritual practice because it didn't look like or feel like any spiritual practice I had ever known before.

My experience in the mountains had shown me that reality was nondual, was One Taste, but it was years before I could return to that understanding with any depth or consistency. I am happy to say that I can now recognize that nondual One Taste more often than not, and I fundamentally feel at home in the world. *Everything* touches me now. Nothing is separate from my own True Self, the infinite feeling of I AM prior to time or causation. It is clear, easy, immediate: *I AM* the world, the world is me, and it is all radiantly, transparently Divine. There is no fallen realm, there is no false or illusory plane of existence. This world *is* the Divine world, and it has always been so. There is *only* infinite Spirit, and I AM That. *All beings* are simply and only That, and it has always been so. Who does not know the simple feeling of I AM? Who is not always-already Enlightened? There is *only* Spirit, and the great nondual spiritual traditions East and West would have us remember and recognize that this is so, has always been so, will always be so. But it was not Zen Buddhism that most profoundly helped me see this truth with consistency. It was not Christian mysticism or Hindu esotericism or the teachings of revered Enlightened Masters passed down for centuries that helped me "get over myself" once and for all. I had studied all of these teachings – that is part of what an Integral Approach recommends – and I had been fundamentally influenced by them (and I still have a great deal more to learn from these Great Wisdom Traditions), but the *practice* that most effectively helped me liberate my attention from separation and division was developed by Scott Ford.

Make no mistake, Scott Ford *is* a Master. He has been developing his teaching for over thirty-seven years, and it is through his thousands of hours on the tennis court that he has come to know his own True Self, that Infinite Identity prior to the Big Bang, that Supreme Being of which this very universe is a perfect gesture. Cannot any activity be prayer if done with devotion and purity of intention? Some mystics dance their way to Realization, some sing, some do yoga, some paint, some write. This mystic plays tennis.

It's not about the action. Many people dance, sing, do yoga, paint, and write—but why? and what for? Are all those who dance Awakened? Certainly not. But what of those who dance for God? What of those who dance *as* God? We would be wise to listen to what those rare souls have to say. In all the great wisdom traditions it is necessary that you *demonstrate* your Awakened understanding. It is not enough to just *say* you are Awakened, you must *show* that you are Awakened through your actions.

Scott Ford teaches how to demonstrate Awakened understanding in tennis (and, in fact, in all sports involving movement. Tennis is a microcosm of human life. There are rules, limits, and consequences—and *within the game* these are *entirely real*, and this is true of everything in the world of manifestation. Perhaps this fact upsets you, and you say, "Forget this, I'm not going to play." That is a choice you are free to make. Some spiritual traditions adopt this attitude rather entirely and their practice is to get into meditative states of consciousness where this world of form drops away entirely—and then they stay there. It's like spending your life in deep-dreamless sleep. There's no fear, no pain, no suffering, because there is *nothing there whatsoever*. It is radically Empty, and there are people who can teach you how to achieve this state on a fairly permanent basis.

Most people, however, want to be a part of the game of living, even amidst a great deal of confusion, disappointment, and pain. So if you've decided you want to be in the game, how are you going to play? Having a temper tantrum about the fact that there are limitations to your experience is simply childish. A tennis court the size of a soccer field would be meaningless; a tennis court without a net is no longer tennis. The boundaries are *necessary* to play the game. This is, in fact, true about everything in the manifest universe. To have any meaning at all, manifest qualities must differentiate from unqualifiable and unmanifest Being. Red cannot be the same color as blue. Depth and width must refer to separate dimensions. Past, present, and future must be logically and chronologically distinct.

A nondual realization shows us that *even though* we are in fact Infinite as unmanifest Awareness without any limitation whatsoever, we *decided* to manifest a universe—we know this because: here it is! So why would Infinity make itself finite, limited, mortal? One answer is that Spirit loves to create, and to create anything you must have boundaries. You must be able to say what your creation is and what it is not. Let's say, as a Divine Being, you wanted to manifest color. Tell me, what is actually more Divine: one Absolute color that retains all qualities of colors within itself? *Or* a near limitless number of distinct, differentiated colors spanning the entire rainbow of possibilities, each and every one shining perfectly as a *unique* expression of Infinite creativity? The nondual mystics throughout history are unanimous: an Absolute that cannot create is decidedly inferior to one that can.

These same mystics are equally unanimous in their declaration that *everyone* without exception participates *perfectly* in the Divine Identity. The Divine *is* you, you *are* the Divine. The Divine *is* creating the universe moment to moment, which is to say, *you* are creating this universe moment to moment. It's *your* game. Emptiness by itself is, shall we say, dull. Literally nothing happens there, and never will. *You*, as Absolute Emptiness, freely chose these apparent limitations, and you chose them because you *wanted* to play. *You* chose this game—so how do you want to play? Like a finite being, trapped, mortal, and terrified of death? Or like a Divine being, who is absolutely *thrilled* at the opportunity to participate in literally the most awesome and mysterious story ever told?

Scott Ford is a Master of teaching us how to play the Divine game we—each and every one of us—*chose* to start. Tennis is a microcosm of the human experience: there are winners and losers, success and failure, astonishing triumphs and crushing defeats. You came here to play. In your heart of hearts, you know this to be true. So *how* do you want to play? What identity will you choose to play with? Finite or Infinite? Mortal or Immortal? Limited or Limitless? It's up to you.

Scott can show you how to be a Divine Being on the tennis court, and if you can see, even once, that it's possible to be Perfectly Free amidst the confusion and chaos of full-blown competition, you will know with absolutely certainty that you can be Free anywhere in your life. This is the astonishing opportunity Scott invites us to explore with him. Get up off your meditation mat and grab a racquet. *Show me* your True Self in action! There is nothing to fear. Life is for the living, and *you chose this game*—so come out and play, and we'll meet you there.

See you on the courts.

Colin Bigelow
Senior Assistant to Ken Wilber

APPENDIX

A Tale of Two Napkins

Early in my journey along this path of sports and spirituality, I had an experience that I can only describe as surreal. It involved NORAD's Department of Astrodynamics, a theoretical mathematician named Felix, and my simple diagram of a contact sequence in tennis. This diagram:

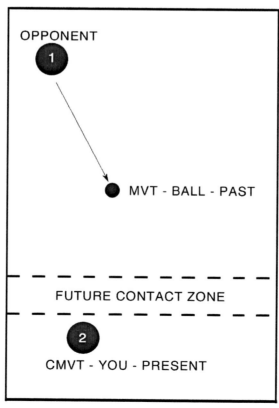

Here's the backstory: One of my tennis students at the time, Ron Roehrich, was the Director of NORAD's Department of Astrodynamics in Colorado Springs, Colorado, where I was teaching tennis at the Colorado Springs Racquet Club. I asked Ron if he would check out the space-time diagram I had come up with to explain how players got in the present by focusing on the future while simultaneously seeing the past. He said he didn't know much about space-time theory but he had one of the best theoretical mathematicians in the country working at his offices, a guy named Felix Hoots. He would have Felix take a look at my diagram, make corrections, and get the corrected diagram back to me the next day.

Two weeks later he contacted me and said Felix couldn't find anything wrong with my diagram and wanted to know how I came up with it. I immediately asked if Felix played tennis, which he did, and the next day Felix was not only playing tennis, he was playing tennis in the zone. After his zone experience, he said, "Let's go to lunch and talk."

This is where it gets surreal. At lunch Felix took his napkin and on it he drew this diagram of time:

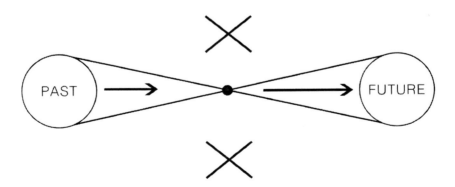

As he was drawing this diagram he mentioned in passing that nothing could exist outside the boundaries of time and pointed to the areas I've marked with an X. From there, our conversation went something like this:

Felix: Have you ever seen this diagram before?

Me: Uh, no…

Felix: It's Einstein's Diagram of Time. How does your diagram relate to his?

See what I mean about surreal? How does my diagram relate to Einstein's? I remember my mind going completely blank, and yet as I looked at the diagram he'd drawn on the napkin, it suddenly struck me that this view of time was similar to the linear view of a contact sequence in time.

MVT → CMVT → CNT

Past → Present → Future

Without hesitation, I said, "This is a diagram of what time looks like in Time," and then I did something inspired purely by the moment. I took the napkin, folded it over from right to left so that only the past time cone was showing. Then I took Felix's pen and drew on the folded napkin a slightly different view of the future time cone. The new diagram on the folded napkin looked like this:

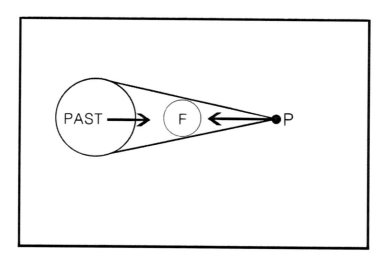

Next I drew a contact sequence diagram on my own napkin and put the two napkins together so they looked like this:

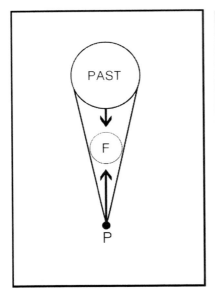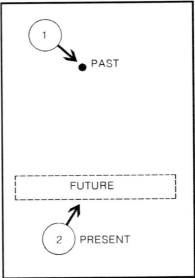

Felix looked for a moment at the two napkins, then his eyes lit up, and to my complete surprise he said something totally unexpected. He said, "RADAR! That looks like RADAR."

Surreal, yes? I'm talking tennis in the zone; he's talking radar!

Later that week I received a letter from "Felix R. Hoots, Mathematician" supporting "further development of my theory." But it wasn't until decades later, after coaching and practicing the zone on a daily basis, and after reading most of the writings of Ken Wilber on the ultimate nature of reality, that I realized the most important part of my lunch meeting with Felix Hoots was not that a theoretical mathematician had found my ideas "intriguing and worth pursuing," but rather what was said in passing when Felix first drew Einstein's diagram of Time and said, "nothing can exist outside the boundaries of Time."

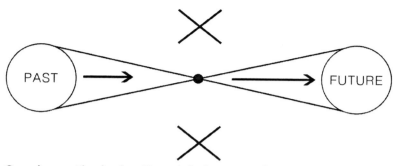

One day, as I looked at Einstein's diagram of Time as Felix had drawn it, I nonchalantly doodled a few changes to the original so it looked like this:

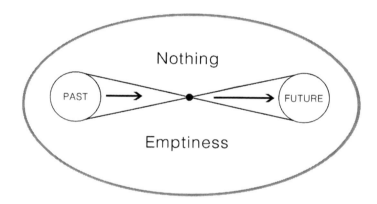

It didn't take long before I realized that I was looking at a diagram that included the relative domain of space and time AND the absolute domain that exists outside the boundaries of space and time – the domain of the Spirit, the domain of the Infinite and Eternal Present. And with that realization, I knew that I was looking at a diagram of the ultimate nature of reality. Metaphorical, yes, but a representation of form arising in emptiness, relative presence arising with and within the Absolute Presence of Eternity.

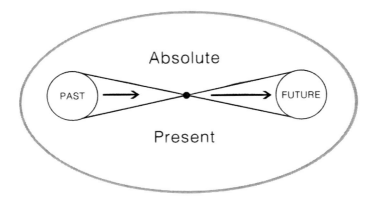

So what does any of this have to do with tennis in the zone or with awakening to your Authentic Self? Just as the Authentic Self only comes out to play in the relative domain of flowing presence, the True Self is always already playing in the Absolute domain of Eternal Presence. And to recognize the Eternal Presence of your True Self, all you have to do is feel into your own presence, your own I AMness, your own simple sense of being. Here's how:

The Wall

I learned to play tennis by hitting tennis balls against a wall – more exactly, a garage door – the garage door of my childhood home in Aurora, Colorado. A one-car, wooden garage door, probably 7 or 8 feet high and about 10 feet across, painted a dull, brownish-red with a handle located just below what would be the height of the net. The driveway leading into the garage had a slight incline and cracks in the concrete, lots of cracks.

It was here that my dad showed his three sons, Pat, Mike, and Scott how to hit a tennis ball with a tennis racquet. His instructions: "This is how you hit a forehand, this is how you hit a backhand, and this is how you hit a serve. There's the garage door. Have fun. When you can hit it a thousand times in a row, we'll go to the courts." (The Thousand Ball Club!)

That was it. That was my introduction to tennis, and it was also my introduction to a lifelong friend and teacher. A friend who was always available to play. A friend who never complained about the playing conditions, never criticized my game, never commented on my form, my footwork, my strengths, or my weaknesses, and yet, the wall was the best teacher I ever had. The only teacher I ever had. And the wall had only one way of teaching, and it was very effective. You see, the wall never missed.

By its very nature, hitting against the wall is a private practice, a time when you can practice getting in the zone, or, more exactly, a time when you can practice presence, and as you learn to maintain and stabilize presence, you also become more conscious of your Authentic Self. Remember, your Authentic Self only comes out to play when you are in the present, and the wall gives you a perfect place to practice the co-creation of flowing presence.

Learning to connect to what is already there – the present dimension – is the deeper purpose for this private practice. The wall provides a consistent practice partner who always returns the ball, and with a little imagination, you can see how the wall plays the same role as your imaginary window. Nothing you hit gets past the wall, and likewise, nothing the wall returns in your direction gets past your imaginary wall/window.

That's it. That's all you do. Use your racquet to keep the ball from getting past your imaginary window, again and again and again. Say "yes" when you are successful. Say "no" when you're not. A simple practice in which presence is both the journey and the destination.

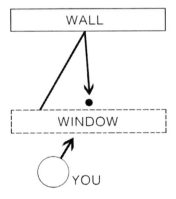

In this private practice the deeper objective is to shift into and maintain a state of flowing presence, and as you stabilize this fully integrated conscious state you will also stabilize your Authentic Self. Operationally, this is done by shifting into FDF's parallel visual interface and continuously locating the contact point on your imaginary window. As you practice using FDF as your visual input pattern in this highly controlled contact sequence environment, not only are you practicing the most efficient and accurate visual input pattern you can use in a fast-moving ball sport such as tennis, but you are also practicing the unified visual and mental pattern of focus that maintains your connection to the flowing present.

With enough time spent in a Parallel Mode of exterior operation with its interior correlate of integral consciousness, and with enough time spent in this controlled and private contact sequence environment, you will begin to shift away from hitting *against the wall* and come to understand that you are actually hitting *with the wall*. No longer will the competition be one of you against the wall, but rather it will become a competition of you and the wall striving together for a higher purpose: the awakening of your Authentic Self to the unified reality of flowing presence.

Question: can this peak experience of unified reality occur in something as simple and ordinary as bouncing a tennis ball off a wall again and again and again?

The answer is a very definitive yes! Unified reality is always present in everything we do. We just don't connect to it very often because we mostly connect to our environment in a Serial Mode of operation, asymmetrically attached to the past dimension of form while ignoring the future dimension of empty space. In tennis, if you focus on the ball or any other object in your visual field, then that asymmetrical connection immediately divides the whole of unified reality into an assortment of incomplete parts. Simply by focusing on form, you unintentionally ignore empty space, and if you only connect to form, then you are only connecting to half of what is available to you in the full potential of unified reality. And a partially potentiated experience is always incomplete, always lacking that *something* you just can't put your finger on. That's when the seeking begins again, only what you're looking for is not lost, it's just not found where you're looking, and the reason you can't put your finger on what's missing in your experience is that you can't put your finger on nothing.

You can, however, put your mind on nothing. You can focus your mind on empty space, and one of the most immediate ways to focus your mind on empty space is to fix the focus of your eyes on the empty space that is, was, and always will be your contact zone.

The wall is the perfect place to practice focusing on empty space as form arises in its moment-to-moment advance.

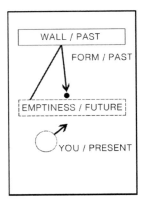

Remember, as you fix your visual and mental focus on your contact zone/window, you will still *see* the wall and you will still *see* the ball, which means you will still *see* the parts as they arise sequentially within the whole of your visual field. As you rest your eyes on empty space and look for the contact point along the surface of your imaginary window, you are visually creating a parallel interface with the immediate past and the immediate future of each arising R-field moment. In short, you are creating a direct connection to the unified reality that is the flowing present dimension.

Immediately upon shifting to a parallel temporal interface, you become one with the here and now of each arising contact sequence, one with the relative present, one with what Christian mystics called the *nunc fluens*, the passing present. And as you become one with the *nunc fluens*, you will find yourself face-to-face with the *nunc stans*, the Eternal and Infinite present moment. Realize that you are not separate from that. You are never separate from the Eternal Now.

Each contact sequence takes time. At contact, what was the present contact sequence becomes the past, and what was the future contact sequence becomes the present. But throughout the moment-to-moment perpetuation of these contact sequences, one thing never changes, one reality is always a constant, and that constant is the Eternal Presence in which each of these contact sequences arises. You can experience these contact sequences in your normal performance state or your peak performance state. Each is a different manifestation of "form in action." Yet both arise on a backdrop of total stillness, absolute emptiness; the absolute emptiness that is Eternal Presence.

Call it Big Mind, call it Buddha Mind, Christ-Consciousness, Absolute Presence, Spirit, God, your Original Face. Call it what you will, it is the unqualifiable emptiness that is the Ground of All Being, the Source of All Becoming. And it is from this Source that all things arise, including you, your states of consciousness, your modes of operation, your functional fit in your athletic environment, even your relationship to the competition itself.

As you continue to hit tennis balls back and forth with the wall, notice how time changes with each passing contact sequence. One R-field moment is completed in space and time, then another, then another. Time passes, things change, you change and novelty occurs. Life goes on, but the one thing that never changes from one contact sequence to the next is your constant sense of presence. That constant sense of presence, that sense of I AMness never changes, even amidst all the variables taking place in each successive contact sequence.

All the movement, all the countermovement, all the positive and negative contact, all these variables are continuously changing in time and space, but the one constant that never changes, the one constant that transcends both time and space, is your constant sense of presence, your perpetual I AMness.

It was there when you first started hitting balls against the wall. It was there in that first contact sequence. It was there in the next contact sequence and the next and the next. Throughout all that change, your I AMness remains changeless. Amidst all those variables in time and space, this I AMness remains the timeless, spaceless constant in which all variables arise.

And it is here right now as your read these words. Your sense of presence is always with you. It is never not present. Think back to when you first started reading this book. What was present? The same, unchanging I AMness was right there with you, always was, always is, and always will be. And as you take up the simple practice of hitting with the wall, as you become one with each and every R-field moment, as you connect to the flowing presence of each arising contact sequence and awaken to your Authentic Self, notice also the underlying stillness in which your Authentic Self arises, stays for a while, then leaves as you return to your egoic state. Notice, too, that no matter what your performance state, normal or peak, that it comes, stays for a while, then leaves again. But what does not leave, what always stays, is the ever-present awareness that is your deepest, True Self.

Recognize that You are that ever-present awareness. You are the emptiness in which all form arises. Everything you relate to, everything you compete against, laugh with, cry with, fear, love, every win and loss that seemingly takes place "out there" separate from you, actually takes place "in here" in your ever-present consciousness. And you are not separate from all that arises in your consciousness. Indeed, you are one with all that arises in your consciousness.

To awaken is to know that you are not separate from anything. Your deepest self, your True Self, is not separate from Eternity, not separate from Infinity, not separate from Spirit, not separate from God.

- You and Spirit are One.
- You and God are One.

All is available to you right here, right now as you recognize the ever-present emptiness in which each contact sequence arises as you hit a little tennis ball back and forth with God.

Instructions

Some basic instructions for hitting with the wall as a practice for shifting into unified, integral consciousness:

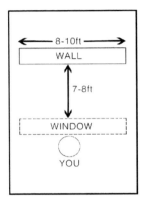

1. Start close to the wall – approximately 7-8 feet away.
2. Use short strokes – the objective in hitting with the wall is to get in the zone, and a short distance between you and the wall combined with short, controllable strokes, makes it easier to learn and maintain a Parallel Mode of operation.
3. Whether you are inside or outside, begin by visualizing a window spanning the area in front of you and use your short strokes to keep the oncoming ball from getting past your imaginary window.

(Note: Use Quick Start tennis balls. These are soft foam tennis balls that won't break anything and can be used indoors or outdoors. They are slightly larger than regular tennis balls, and, most importantly, they are QUIET! You can also find any number of Quick Start racquets that are smaller and easier to use than a full-sized tennis racquet. Remember, this is not as much about tennis as it is about maintaining a state of integral consciousness. The Quick Start equipment is the easiest to use and the least expensive to buy.)

Essentially, you and the wall are doing the same thing. By visualizing an imaginary window in front of you, you are creating an imaginary wall to represent your contact zone. An invisible wall or a window on which to rest your focus and through which you can observe the ball as it moves back and forth from wall to window to wall to window.

Keep in mind that you can *see* the ball without *focusing* on the ball. In fact, you can see everything arising in your visual field without focusing on any of the individual parts. So the concentrative task is simple: visualize a window in front of you and defend it from oncoming balls. Say "yes" if you keep the ball from breaking through your window, say "no" if you don't.

That's it. That's all you do. And do it as many times in a row as you can – without missing. Remember, you have to earn your membership to the Thousand Ball Club! So maintain your focus for as long as you can. Resist the temptation to focus on the ball as it goes back and forth between your window and the wall. Instead, remain focused on your window as the ball comes into focus and then goes out of focus. "Yes/ No" feedback helps keep you on task.

As you become more proficient in this private wall practice, you will also develop an increased awareness of contact, a deeply conscious awareness of exactly what occurs at the contact point on your imaginary window. This increasing awareness of contact comes with your increasing presence at the event of contact itself. You will develop contact awareness by simply saying "yes" *at the exact moment of contact.* Not before contact, not after contact, but at exactly the moment the movement of the ball and the countermovement of your racquet come together at a common point along the surface of your window, a common point in space and time wherein the past, the present, and the future come together to create the perfect point of presence. The uniquely singular point at which the old contact sequence dies as it gives birth to a new contact sequence. The point at which the categories of the ultimate are displayed in their most fundamental form: the many, the one, and the ultimate of ultimates – the creative advance into novelty.

Again and again and again. Contact, contact, contact. Right here – right now, right here – right now. Are you here? Are you now? Are you present with the perfect moment of presence? Are you one with contact?

Contact awareness is present moment awareness; awareness of the here and now exactly where and when it happens. Be completely present at contact, again and again, and you will realize that you are not separate from that finite moment. You are never separate from the now moment. The real you, the authentic you, is never separate from the here and now. Your egoic self, however, your small self, is always separated from the present, always flip-flopping back and forth between past and future, then and there. Never present, never here, never now.

Hitting with the wall is a practice that can awaken you to present moment awareness, and that awareness can be recognized repeatedly as you say "yes" at the exact now moment of contact.

The practice: visualize an imaginary window in front of you and use your racquet to keep the oncoming ball from getting past your window. Say "yes" when you are successful. Say "no" when you aren't. One contact sequence at a time. One contact event at a time. One moment of total presence followed by another, then another – again and again and again. And as you look into the face of presence, realize that you are looking at your own deepest face, your own original face, the face you had before the beginning of time. And that face, your Original Face, is the Infinite face of Eternity.

Glossary

Contact Point: simultaneously the Omega Point of the past contact sequence (Old R-Field) and the Alpha Point of the presently arising contact sequence (New R-field).

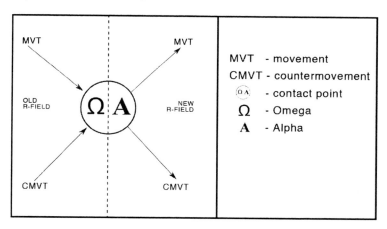

Contact Sequence: the fundamental sequence of all sports involving contact – such as tennis, baseball, golf, etc.

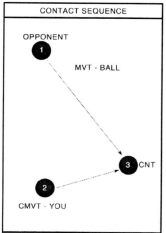

First comes the Movement of the ball, followed by your Countermovement to intercept the ball, ending with Contact – the event that occurs when Movement and Countermovement come together at a common point in space and time.

Every contact sequence has an *absolute nature* that never changes and a *relative nature* that is always changing.

With contact, the individual parts come together to create a unified whole.

Dorsal Visual Pathway: The dorsal system passes from the primary visual cortex to the posterior parietal region and functions in visually guiding our moment to moment actions. It codes information in a faster, view-specific way.

Fixed-Depth of Focus Input Pattern (FDF): a parallel input pattern in which your fix the focus of your eyes on your contact zone and locate the contact point of the oncoming object of movement along that fixed-focal plane. Think of it as locating the contact point along the surface of your imaginary window. With FDF input you are inputting parallel streams of visual information about the contact zone *and* the movement of the ball equally and simultaneously. As you keep your contact zone "in focus" you simultaneously see the action in your visual field arising in its moment-to-moment procession. FDF is the visual input pattern of your Peak Performance State. FDF is inherently a parallel input pattern.

Flash-outs: any shift of focus away from your contact zone and your visual objective of locating the Primary contact point along the fixed focal plane of your contact zone. For instance, while focused on your contact zone you might "flash-out" on the oncoming ball, or your opponent, or your target.

Gross Consciousness: an interior state of consciousness in which you are aware of the individual parts of your environment as they arise sequentially in their moment-to-moment procession. An interior state of gross consciousness has as its exterior correlate a Serial Mode of sensorimotor operation.

Integral Consciousness: an interior state of consciousness in which you are aware of the whole of your environment as the parts arise in their moment-to-moment procession. An interior state of integral consciousness has as its exterior correlate a Parallel Mode of sensorimotor operation.

Parallel Mode: an exterior mode of operation in which the sensorimotor operating system connects equally and simultaneously to form and empty space in a parallel interface. A Parallel Mode of exterior operation has as its interior correlate a unified state of integral consciousness.

Relativity Fields (R-fields): the spatiotemporal fields in which and with which you co-create your moment-to-moment reality.

In the relative domain of space-time, form is seen in the movement of the ball, your opponent, the court or field on which you perform, etc. Form, relative to you in your present space, is the immediate past.

Empty space is seen in your contact zone. Empty space, relative to you in your present space, is the immediate future.

In a Serial Mode of operation, your sensorimotor operating system connects individually and sequentially to the objects of movement (past) in your R-field environment by means of a VDF input pattern (focusing on the ball).

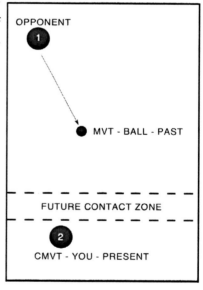

In a Parallel Mode of operation, your sensorimotor operating system connects equally and simultaneously to the contact zone (future) and the object of movement (past) by means of a FDF input pattern (locating the contact point on a fixed-focal plane).

Release Sequence: the fundamental sequence of all sports involving releasing an object – such as shooting a basketball, throwing a baseball, pitching a horseshoe. With release the unified whole divides to create the individual parts.

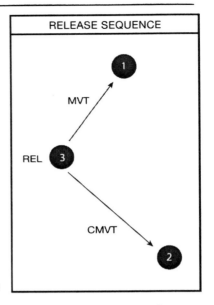

Serial Mode: an exterior mode of operation in which the sensorimotor operating system connects sequentially to form, ignoring empty space, in a dualistic interface. A Serial Mode of exterior operation has as its interior correlate a dualistic state of gross consciousness.

Variable-Depth of Focus Input Pattern (VDF): a serial input pattern in which you focus your eyes on the individual objects in your visual field in a sequential or serial manner. The most recognizable application of VDF in sports is "watching the ball," or "focusing on your opponent." VDF input requires you to continuously refocus your eyes to keep the ball "in focus" as the action in your visual field arises. VDF is the visual input pattern of your Normal Performance State. VDF is inherently a serial input pattern.

Ventral Visual Pathway: The ventral system passes from the primary visual cortex to the inferior temporal lobe, and provides the visual contents of our perceptual experience. It codes information in an abstract form for use in cognitive processes like object recognition and imagining.

Bibliography

Gallwey, W. Timothy. *The Inner Game of Tennis*. Toronto: Bantam, 1979. Print.

Jackson, Susan A., and Mihaly Csikszentmihalyi. *Flow in Sports: The Keys to Optimal Experiences and Performances*. Champaign, IL: Human Kinetics, 1999. Print.

Krug, Matthew. "Playing Tennis in the Zone." *Athletic Insight*. Accessed 28 Mar 2012. <http://www.athleticinsight.com/Vol1Iss3/Tennis_Zone.htm>. Web.

Merzel, Dennis Genpo. *Big Mind, Big Heart: Finding Your Way*. Salt Lake City, UT: Big Mind Publishing, 2007. Print.

Whitehead, Alfred N. *Process and Reality*. Corrected ed. New York: Free Press, 1978. Print.

Wilber, Ken. No Boundary: Eastern and Western Approaches to Personal Growth. Boston: Shambhala, 2001. Print.